OECD Public Governance Reviews

Citizens' Voice in Jordan

THE ROLE OF PUBLIC COMMUNICATION AND MEDIA FOR A MORE OPEN GOVERNMENT

This document, as well as any data and map included herein, are without prejudice to the status of or sovereignty over any territory, to the delimitation of international frontiers and boundaries and to the name of any territory, city or area.

Please cite this publication as:
OECD (2021), *Citizens' Voice in Jordan: The Role of Public Communication and Media for a More Open Government*, OECD Public Governance Reviews, OECD Publishing, Paris, *https://doi.org/10.1787/da85277c-en*.

ISBN 978-92-64-36485-1 (print)
ISBN 978-92-64-89571-3 (pdf)

OECD Public Governance Reviews
ISSN 2219-0406 (print)
ISSN 2219-0414 (online)

Photo credits: Cover designed by Mohamad Sabra; © Maksim Kabakou – Fotolia.com; © Arthimedes/Shutterstock.com; © Peshkova/Shutterstock.com; © Svilen_mitkov/Shutterstock.com.

Corrigenda to publications may be found on line at: *www.oecd.org/about/publishing/corrigenda.htm*.
© OECD 2021

The use of this work, whether digital or print, is governed by the Terms and Conditions to be found at *http://www.oecd.org/termsandconditions*.

Foreword

Public communication is an important tool of government policy and contributor to the open government principles of transparency, integrity, accountability and stakeholder participation. By developing the capacities, processes, and procedures for robust internal and external communication, governments can ensure that information flows both from and within entities in a transparent manner to inform other constituencies of key policy priorities. Likewise, a well-functioning media and information-enabling environment can ensure that information flows in an optimal manner, that major policy issues are publically debated, and that the implementation of government policies is properly monitored and evaluated.

Jordan has given a high priority to enhancing public communication efforts by government agencies. These aspirations have been translated to commitments aimed at opening a dialogue between the State and the public in a host of government plans, including the *Jordan 2025 Vision*, the *National Renaissance Plan* (2019-2020), the Indicative Executive Program (2021-2023) and the Government Economic Recovery Priorities Plan, among others. Led by the Ministry of State for Media Affairs (MoSMA), the central communications entity within the Prime Ministry, the Government is embarking on a restructuring of the public communications function by professionalising communication structures and processes. In so doing, Jordan is taking steps to establish a strategic approach to public communication, which will be crucial as the country faces economic and socio-political challenges.

As the Government of Jordan continues to restructure and strengthen its public communication capacities, it will need to consolidate the progress achieved to date by further institutionalising internal and external communication processes. Empowering public communicators with the right tools and skills will be critical for the successful implementation of Jordan's robust economic, decentralisation and open government reform agendas. At the same time, ensuring a well-functioning media and information-enabling environment will be all the more important to raise awareness and promote an open and constructive debate around key policy issues.

To support the government's efforts, this review was undertaken in the framework of the MENA-OECD Governance Programme and as part of a broader regional project, "Citizens' Voice: Enhancing Open Government through Public Communication and Media Ecosystems". The findings build on similar analyses of practices, challenges, and lessons learned in Lebanon, Morocco, and Tunisia, and reflect Jordan's many achievements as part of its four Open Government Partnership national action plans as well as its efforts to empower stakeholders at all levels of government.

This publication was approved by the OECD Working Party on Open Government on 15 October 2021 and declassified by the Public Governance Committee on 18 November 2021.

Acknowledgements

This report *Citizens' Voice in Jordan: The Role of Public Communication and Media for a More Open Government* was prepared by the OECD Directorate for Public Governance (GOV), under the leadership of its Director, Elsa Pilichowski. The analysis, findings, and recommendations were developed by GOV's Open and Innovative Government Division (OIG), under the strategic direction of Alessandro Bellantoni, Head of the Open Government Unit.

This report was co-ordinated by Karine Badr and was drafted by Michael Jelenic and Paulina López Ramos, with contributions from Rebecca Kachmar. Sophie Le Corre and Elena Martin Gomez-Tembleque provided administrative support throughout the development of the publication. The report was also edited and prepared for publication by Meral Gedik.

The Secretariat wishes to express its gratitude to the government of Jordan, who made this report possible, in particular Jordan's Ministry of State for Media Affairs (MoSMA). The OECD would also like to acknowledge the important contributions to the surveys and the fact-finding missions by a number of public institutions in Jordan, including the Ministries of Transport, Labour; Justice, Awqaf and Religious Affairs, Tourism, Entrepreneurship and Digital Economy, Higher Education, Education, Trade and Industry, Planning and International Cooperation, Health, Culture, as well as the Jordan Investment Commission and the Social Security Corporation. The OECD would also like to thank Kristina Plavšak Krajnc, former Director of the Government Communication Office of Slovenia, for her valuable support as peer reviewer throughout this process.

Finally, the OECD would like to thank the German Federal Foreign Office for its financial support for this project.

Table of contents

Foreword	3
Acknowledgements	4
Executive summary	9
1 Context, assessment, and recommendations	**11**
Introduction	12
Public communication in Jordan	12
Media and information ecosystem in Jordan	13
OECD analytical framework	15
Summary of main findings and recommendations	17
Methodology	22
References	24
Notes	25
2 Communicating for a more open government in Jordan	**27**
Global and regional context	28
OECD Analytical Framework	29
Role of public communication and media in the open government reform process	30
Public communication and media support for open government principles	32
Communicating for an open government in Jordan	37
References	40
Notes	41
3 Improving the governance of public communication in Jordan	**43**
Introduction	44
Recommendations	63
References	64
Notes	66
4 Developing more strategic use of key communication competencies in Jordan	**67**
Introduction	68
Utilising audience insights to maximise reach and impact	69
Leveraging the interactivity benefits of digital communication	70
Evaluating the impact of public communication	76
Recommendations	79
References	80
Notes	81

5 Leveraging the media and information ecosystem in Jordan — 83
Structural issues affecting access to media and information — 84
Institutional issues affecting access to media and information — 89
Stakeholder issues affecting access to media and information — 97
Recommendations — 104
References — 106
Notes — 109

FIGURES

Figure 1.1. OECD framework on public communication — 16
Figure 2.1. Internal and external dimensions of public communication — 31
Figure 2.2. Media and the public policy cycle — 32
Figure 2.3. Public communication provisions of the OECD Recommendation on open government — 37
Figure 3.1. Types of communication structures in Jordanian ministries — 47
Figure 3.2. Types of appointments in Jordanian line ministries — 48
Figure 3.3. Rate of co-ordination on core communication functions in Jordanian Ministries — 50
Figure 3.4. Most important objectives of public communication strategies from line ministries in Jordan — 55
Figure 3.5. Share of ministries in Jordan that receive communication specific training — 58
Figure 3.6. Number of Ministries in Jordan with a dedicated budget for public communication — 62
Figure 4.1. Share of ministries in Jordan selecting the below challenges to implementing core communication competencies — 68
Figure 4.2. Criteria used by Jordanian public institutions for the selection of public communication channels — 69
Figure 4.3. Social media use by Ministries in Jordan — 72
Figure 4.4. Share of Jordanian Ministries partnering with the below stakeholders to boost the reach of digital communication activities — 75
Figure 4.5. Average frequency of the evaluation of public communication competencies by ministries in Jordan — 77
Figure 5.1. Core ICT indicators in Jordan 2010-19 — 85
Figure 5.2. Internet access by sub-districts, 2010-16 — 86
Figure 5.3. Household income by quintile — 87
Figure 5.4. Documents made publically available, per ministry in Jordan — 92
Figure 5.5. Types of documents used for guiding Ministry's response to mis- anddis-information — 95
Figure 5.6. Ministries with an official spokesperson — 101
Figure 5.7. Frequency of press conferences and press releases in Jordanian ministries — 102

TABLES

Table 3.1. Features of tactical and strategic governance models of public communication — 44
Table 4.1. Mapping the online presence of Jordanian Public Institutions — 70
Table 4.2. Government use of Facebook and Twitter in Jordan (2020) — 73
Table 5.1. Global Centre for Law and Democracy: Global Right to Information Rating in Jordan — 91
Table 5.2. Jordan's media and information enabling environment, 2015-20 — 94

Follow OECD Publications on:

- http://twitter.com/OECD_Pubs
- http://www.facebook.com/OECDPublications
- http://www.linkedin.com/groups/OECD-Publications-4645871
- http://www.youtube.com/oecdilibrary
- http://www.oecd.org/oecddirect/

Executive summary

In Jordan, recent transformations to the media and online spheres have affected the availability of information, how information is shared, and the main sources trusted by the public. These developments have prompted a whole-of-government reform of internal and external public communication processes with the aim of addressing citizens' changing needs and expectations. Reinforcing this transition toward a more strategic model can ultimately help ensure optimal flows of information, the active involvement of the media, as well as the open and productive debate of key policy issues.

While much has been achieved through the restructuring of public communication in Jordan, evidence suggests that this function remains underutilised as an instrument for openness and policy-making. Surveyed ministries highlight the absence of skilled staff, financial resources, co-ordination, and established procedures as the reasons behind the reactive nature of communications. Moreover, there is scope for repositioning this function as a two-way engagement mechanism: less than one-third of ministries consider promoting participation as a priority objective of communications and engagement with the media occurs on an ad hoc basis. Addressing these challenges has become ever more urgent. The ongoing COVID-19 pandemic demonstrates the critical importance of clear communications and transparent flows of information for crisis response efforts.

This review provides an analysis and recommendations on how the Government of Jordan can make strategic use of public communication and strengthen the media and information-enabling environment. This report first takes stock of the main related developments in Jordan and establishes a framework of how public communication can contribute to open government reforms. Subsequently, the report provides an analysis and recommendations for adopting a more strategic use of public communication by institutionalising and professionalising core structures, processes and competencies. Finally, this review identifies opportunities for the government to more effectively engage with citizens by creating an environment that supports the media and information sharing.

Improving the governance of public communication in Jordan

Public communication structures, processes, and mandates in Jordan could be further institutionalised to help government entities engage with the public in more proactive and strategic ways. At present, such structures vary significantly in terms of their organisation, functioning, and level of resources, in some cases relying on the work of a single individual. At the same time, a variety of arrangements contribute to the uneven and uncoordinated application of activities, exacerbated in turn by the lack of an overarching communication strategy as well as limited human and financial resources.

To address these challenges, the OECD suggests several ways to strengthen governance arrangements and support the effectiveness of internal government operations. First, efforts will be needed to standardise structures and formalize procedures to ensure the consistency of the role and mandate of public communicators. Second, professionalising media units will also require technical training and the establishment of dedicated budgets to implement new restructuring directives, which could be monitored through a whole-of-government strategy. Finally, the reactivated network of public communicators could serve as a platform to improve co-ordination and secure buy-in from the political leadership to allocate resources for this function.

Developing a more strategic use of key communication competencies in Jordan

Professionalising core capabilities in government institutions is needed both to establish a two-way dialogue with the public and strengthen internal processes. Overall, OECD survey results reveal that the skills and competencies most lacking in Jordanian ministries include effectively deploying campaigns, producing communication strategies, engaging through digital channels, and evaluating impact. While there is no one-size-fits-all approach, setting an established methodology, creating centres of expertise and equipping public entities with the right tools and skills will be central to addressing the *ad hoc* and uneven implementation of activities in these areas.

In order to address these challenges, the OECD provides several recommendations to strengthen key communication capabilities. First, promoting the collection and use of insights from target audiences can help governments better understand the most favoured means of communication and identify messages that have the most impact on citizens. Second, there is potential to standardise the use of digital channels and promote their role as interfaces for stakeholder participation, given the high internet and social media penetration rates in the country. Finally, the establishment of a consistent evaluation methodology, assessing impact metrics and baselines, can help measure performance and better inform future communications.

Leveraging the media and information ecosystem in Jordan

A sound and well-regulated media and information-enabling environment is vitally important for communicating a variety of pertinent policy priorities. However, a number of political economy challenges hamper the effective use of the media and information ecosystem to support Jordan's strategic communications efforts. At a structural level, these include a growing digital divide between urban and rural areas as well as among key segments of the population. Likewise, at an institutional level, challenges include a highly complex legal framework with numerous—and sometimes overlapping—laws, directives, and regulations governing how media and broadcast organisations as well as online outlets can function. Finally, with respect to the various stakeholders involved, challenges include difficulties in the accreditation of journalists, the need for greater plurality and independence of media outlets, the need for greater transparency in the licencing process, capacity challenges for government spokespeople engaging the media, and the changing demographics of media consumers.

To meet these challenges, the OECD offers several recommendations that can support a robust media and information-enabling environment. With regard to structural challenges, strategic channel selection and audience insights are needed in order to tailor content to the context of specific audience needs and support greater media and information literacy capabilities. Likewise, to address institutional challenges, a review of the current legal framework is needed to ensure consistency among laws, regulations, directives, and policies, with an aim to align them with international good practices is crucial. Finally, to address stakeholder challenges, support is needed for increasing the reach of media outlets at the local level, expanding journalist accreditation procedures, supporting the plurality and independence of media outlets, developing an ombudsman or independent complaints mechanism, and building the media literacy of government agencies, CSOs, and citizens.

1 Context, assessment, and recommendations

This chapter provides an overview of the main legal and institutional changes that have affected the state of public communication in Jordan, including the recent growth of the media and information sector. It then presents the OECD's framework for open government, public communication, and media ecosystems, which will be analysed in depth in subsequent chapters of the report. The chapter ends with a summary of the main conclusions and recommendations of the report concerning the governance of public communication, the strategic use of core capacities, and opportunities to promote a sound media and information enabling environment in the country.

Introduction

Over the last twenty years, Jordan has pursued a path of gradual modernisation and reform that has accelerated since the 2011 Arab Spring, which called for greater voice in public decisions. In response, King Abdullah II established a Royal Committee and the National Dialogue Committee to identify reform priorities and engage in meaningful discussions with the public. As a result of these deliberations, 42 articles in the Constitution were amended and a National Integrity and Anti-Corruption Commission was formed in 2016. In 2007, the adoption of the Access to Information (ATI) Law (No. 47 of 2007), the first in the Arab region, set a key milestone towards opening up Jordan's government.

The country's regional leadership in promoting an open government agenda also highlights its reform progress, as evidenced by it being the first Arab country to join the Open Government Partnership (OGP) in 2011. As part of these efforts, Jordan has undertaken four OGP National Action Plans and, in collaboration with the OECD, it established an Open Government Unit within the Ministry of Planning and International Co-operation (MOPIC) in May 2018. The fourth and current OGP Plan (2018-2020) involved an inclusive design process, led by MOPIC's survey of over 170 stakeholders about priorities for open government initiatives. These efforts were complemented by online consultations and public comment sessions of the draft commitments.

Despite this progress, Jordan's progress on governance and social reforms has been challenged by a difficult economic and geopolitical context. In 2019, the rate of economic growth slowed significantly from an expected rate of 5% to 2.2% in real terms (Kardoosh, 2019[1]). Fiscal pressures in the country can be linked to mounting regional challenges, most visibly the crisis in Syria and, prior to that, Iraq, which have "caused influxes of refugees that have strained health and education services and disrupted trade routes" (World Bank, 2019[2]). This slowdown may be further exacerbated by the Coronavirus (COVID-19) pandemic, which has considerably "weakened Jordan's short and mid-term growth prospects" (World Bank, 2020[3]).

The unfavourable economic context has motivated some discontent among Jordanians, as expressed in recent demonstrations. Indeed, a series of protests throughout 2018 and 2019 were sparked in part by IMF-backed austerity measures aimed at tackling the country's public debt. This is in parallel taking place alongside declining levels of trust, with 72% of Jordanians reporting a lack of confidence in the Parliament (International Republican Institute, 2018[4]). Accordingly, this backdrop makes effective public communication an important asset for Jordan to establish a better dialogue with citizens, allow them to participate, and, ultimately, achieve greater buy-in over policy changes and build trust among citizens.

This chapter will provide an overview of the main findings and recommendations of the OECD Review *"Citizens' Voice in Jordan: The Role of Public Communication and Media for a More Open Government"*. In doing so, it will first take stock of the main developments shaping the Jordanian context, including those pertaining to the public communication function and broader media reform. The chapter will then outline an analytical framework on how public communication and a sound media ecosystem can contribute to promoting the principles of transparency, accountability, integrity and stakeholder participation. Subsequently, it will summarise the key recommendations for the Government of Jordan to strengthen the governance of the public communication function, professionalise core communication competencies and foster a sound media ecosystem.

Public communication in Jordan

The Government acknowledges the potential and urgency of engaging with citizens, and it has identified public communication as a key element of its reform agenda. In a 2018 public message, King Abdullah II acknowledged that "governments are compelled to work transparently and provide accurate, timely information to the public in this era of openness." (King Abdullah II ibn Al Hussein, 2018[5]). In this op-ed, the King emphasised the benefits of social media platforms, but also the need to respond to the challenges they pose, in particular those related to hate speech and disinformation.

Similarly, communication was included as a priority within a host of Government Plans providing a roadmap for policy reform, including the Jordan 2025 Vision, the National Renaissance Plan (2019-2020), the Indicative Executive Program (2021–2023), and the forthcoming Government Economic Recovery Priorities Plan, among others. The Plan included provisions to strengthen freedom of expression and acknowledged public communication as a lever to deliver policy outcomes by "providing channels of communication between citizen and government to ensure transparency, openness and accountability" (Government of Jordan, 2018[6]). Overall, the Plan's aim is to increase public sector transparency, accountability and integrity, as well as foster greater participation and dialogue, all of which are indicative of a greater focus on open government policies.

The Open Government Unit in MOPIC and Jordan's OGP action plans have also reflected the government's commitments to better communication and stronger media ecosystems. The Kingdom's third OGP National Action Plan (2016-18) included two commitments focused on supporting the legislative framework governing access to information and freedom of the media, respectively. Furthermore, the development process of Jordan's fourth OGP National Action Plan (2018-2020) put in practice many effective communication and engagement practices, as MOPIC leveraged channels of communication to produce the most inclusive and consultative document to date. The process saw over 2 000 Facebook engagements; 269 participants in meetings and consultation sessions; and 145 responses to the opinion poll and call for public comments. This activity exemplifies the potential for communications approaches to drive better and more inclusive policymaking.

To support these public communication efforts, government programmes benefit from a well-established institutional and organisational framework. Consolidating itself as a central hub, the Ministry of State for Media Affairs (MoSMA) leads public communication policy and supports the work of media units across ministries. Likewise, the government has established a network of public communicators, known as the *Shabakat Al Natiqeen fil Wuzaraat wa'al Muasasaat al Hukumiya Al Urduniya*, translated literally as "Network of Spokespersons in the Ministries and Institutions of the Government of Jordan." Through this network, the government seeks to reinforce the capacities of spokespeople in key ministries, departments, and agencies as well as to co-ordinate messaging across ministries, departments, and agencies.

In addition to these efforts, the government has worked to develop institutional responses to disinformation and misinformation. In this regard, Jordan has established a disinformation platform, "Haggak Tiraf" ("You have the Right to Know"), which aims to verify the information presented in news stories and social media to prevent the spread of rumours and disinformation. The platform aims to deliver information and necessary clarifications—or in the case of false or misleading information, to refute claims—in an effort to provide timely, accurate, and reliable information, and in a larger sense, to restore citizens' trust in the government.

Media and information ecosystem in Jordan

A diverse media ecosystem is an essential element of open societies, as it enables journalists to amplify the reach of government information, hold the government to account and represent citizens' voices. In this regard, a sound media landscape calls for the empowerment of a wide diversity of voices, ranging from public, private and commercial news and information providers to those at the very grass root level such as community media and citizen journalism. Acknowledging its important role, Jordan has placed media reform high on its agenda over the last decade. Key political events, such as the 1989 demonstrations, the beginning of the reign of King Abdullah II in 1999, and the 2011 Arab Spring, together with the emergence of digital communications technologies, have prompted Jordan to undertake a gradual transformation of its media sector.

Jordan's media enabling environment is rooted in a well-established legal framework, including Article 15 of the Jordanian Constitution of 1952, which grants the freedoms of expression, opinion, and the press. Similarly, Jordan's first regulations of the media date back to the April 1989 demonstrations, which resulted in the introduction of the Press and Publications Law (No. 8 of 1993), leading to the establishment of several private newspapers. A subsequent Press and Publications Law in 1998 (No. 8 of 1998)[1] further helped to expand the sector but also introduced higher capital requirements for new media outlets (Jones, 2001[7]). In parallel, the Jordan Press Association (JPA) was established in 1953 and tasked with regulating professional journalism and serving as a union for its members according to directives of the amended Press Association Law (No. 15 of 1998) (Alisal, 2015[8]).

In 2002, a second wave of media reforms was included within the country's national strategy. Notably, this sweeping policy agenda promoted by King Abdullah II aimed to strengthen parliamentary democracy, the rule of law, media freedom, government accountability, transparency, justice and equal rights. In practice, this saw the end of the state monopoly on radio and television broadcasting with the introduction of the Audio-Visual Law (No. 71 of 2002). The subsequent emergence of new radio and television stations considerably increased the diversity of media outlets in Jordan, which were brought under the regulation of the newly-established Audio-Visual Commission (UNESCO, 2015[9]). In addition, the Press and Publications law and the 2007 ATI Law also offered Jordan's media an additional tool for more transparent reporting through concrete regulatory provisions safeguarding this right for the media and the general public more broadly (Ibid).

The media ecosystem in Jordan underwent further transformations in the aftermath of the 2011 Arab Spring demonstrations. Online platforms and social media became essential means to disseminate information and reach wider segments of the population (Alkhatib, 2017[10]). In March 2011, King Abdullah II delivered a royal address urging the government to develop a "media strategy" to respond to the new opportunities and challenges brought about by technological advancements in communications (UNESCO, 2015[9]) The resulting Jordan Media Strategy (2011-2015) emphasised the important role of media and journalism in society and set out a reform agenda to meet the emerging issues that concerned the sector. A product of a cross-ministerial committee,[2] the strategy's main provisions underscored the importance of adapting regulations to the new types of media in Jordan, updating standards for professional journalism and promoting media self-regulation (for instance, through codes of conduct). Moreover, the development of the strategy involved an extensive consultation process that brought together public, private and community media stakeholders (UNESCO, 2015[9]).[3]

The strategy translated into a number of legislative amendments, including topics related to press and publications, the protection of state secrets and documents, broadcasting and access to information. These changes reflected an effort to adapt legal frameworks to a new media landscape increasingly dominated by digital platforms (United Nations, 2013[11]). For instance, the 2012 Press and Publications Law introduced a series of requirements, such as for news websites to obtain a government license. It similarly extended the law's content restrictions to online publications. The law governing the JPA was also revised in 2014 and extended its membership to "include journalists working at news websites or in the newsrooms of private television and radio stations (UNESCO, 2015[9])". Further amendments updating the regulatory framework led to the creation of the Jordan Media Commission in 2014 as a public body tasked with overseeing the licensing and regulation of the sector (Mediterranean Network of Regulatory Authorities, n.d.[12]).

Subsequent governments have reacted to emerging threats relating to terrorism and cybercrime linked to the surge in online media and content. Notably, the 2011 Cyber Crimes Law and 2014 amendments to the Anti-Terrorism Law, while seeking to address security challenges, have had the effect of "broadening the grey area over what online content can be restricted" (Freedom House, 2017[13]). Broadly, these transformations have led to a liberalisation and diversification of the media landscape under an evolving legal and institutional framework.

Most recently, in an effort to improve citizens' ability to critically consume and share news, the Minister of Culture launched the *National Executive Plan on Media and Information Literacy (2020-2023)* on 17 June 2020 (Jordan Times, 2020[14]). In addition to the Indicative Executive Program (2021–2023) and the forthcoming Government Economic Recovery Priorities Plan, the National Executive Plan on Media and Information Literacy sets out a programme to improve citizens' ability to deal with information, news sources and digital tools, including a particular focus on empowering youth to discern disinformation, rumours and hate speech. As part of the commitments therein, the Ministry of Culture introduced an online portal called "Our Trust" to provide cultural and training resources in media literacy, ongoing briefings on the opportunities offered by the plan in schools, universities, or civil society organisations, as well as a series of educational videos.

As a result of the aforementioned legislative and institutional developments, Jordan's print, broadcast, radio, and online outlets are relatively diverse, and have increased over time due to liberalised laws and fewer regulatory restrictions. Key private and public media outlets include 21 press institutions operating in the country—nine daily, nine weekly, and three monthly newspapers—as well as 122 licensed online news websites as of 2019 and close to 180 in total as of 2021 (The Jordan Times, 2019[15]). For their part, television broadcast outlets have likewise grown in Jordan. Currently, 45 satellite television channels operate in Jordan, 17 of which are owned by and directed at Jordanians, 15 of which are private, and two of which are public (UNESCO, 2015, p. 105[9]). Radio remains an important channel of broadcast in Jordan, both at the national and regional levels, with 37 FM radio stations operating in Jordan, including three international channels (UNESCO, 2015, p. 27[9]).

The evolution of the media ecosystem in the country has also affected the ways in which the public consumes, communicates and shares information in favour of online channels. Notably, Jordan has a high internet penetration rate more than half of the population actively using WhatsApp (78%), Facebook (70%) and YouTube (49%) (Internet World Statistics, 2018[16]). Television (88%) and smartphones (77%) are the most popular channels for Jordanians to consult the news, in addition to a growing share who use Facebook (41%), YouTube (28%) and WhatsApp (24%) for this purpose (NorthWestern University, 2017[17]). These trends are all the more important when it comes to young people. With youth (aged 12-30) accounting for more than one-third of the population, Jordan is one of the youngest countries in the world (OECD Development Centre, 2018[18]). As in most OECD countries, social media has become a primary vehicle for engaging with youth, as a significant majority of the target group aged between 18-22 makes use of WhatsApp (82%), Facebook (82%), YouTube (63%) and Instagram (57%) (Northwestern University, 2018[19]).

OECD analytical framework

Many OECD countries have begun to leverage open government reforms to address these critical governance challenges. One critical avenue to facilitate these open government principles is through the use of effective public communication and government engagement with media and information enabling environment. Accordingly, this report seeks to explore the role of communication and media as levers for more open governments, inclusive policymaking, and improved service design and delivery, which can ultimately help restore trust and facilitate inclusive growth.

In doing so, the OECD has identified three pillars of effective public communication that can serve as policy catalysts to bring about a set of desired medium- and long-term outcomes, while building on and reinforcing open government principles (see Figure 1.1).

- **Institutional and Governance Arrangements:** In order for public communication to effectively advance open government principles and serve as a tool to improve policymaking and service design and delivery, it is necessary to ensure that certain institutional and governance prerequisites are in place. In particular, to ensure effective public communication across and between levels of government, it is necessary to introduce mechanisms to co-ordinate public communications functions, including horizontally (across sectors and ministries) and vertically (across levels of government). To facilitate this, results-based strategies and communications plans should be developed based on audience insights, strong M&E systems, and feedback loops to ensure an iterative approach that builds on both past success and failures alike. At the same time, a network of public communications actively engaged in the process is necessary to ensure co-ordination, exchange good practices, as well as to help professionalise the role of government communicators. Finally, the necessary human and financial resources should be in place to better support the public communications function across government.

- **Core Communications Competencies and Capacities:** In addition to having the relevant governance mechanisms in place, it is vital to ensure the development of core communication competencies with an open government focus. This includes, among others, developing audience insights and channels; executing campaigns to achieve strategic objectives; engaging digital communications, including social media; as well as building capacities for crisis communication. These competencies, when applied well, can expand the use of public communication from an information dissemination tool, to a lever of stakeholder participation, policy implementation, as well as improved service design and delivery.

- **Robust Media and Information Enabling Environment:** A final pillar to ensure effective public communication is the existence of a robust and well-functioning media and information enabling environment. To assess the potential role that media as well as the larger enabling environment can play in the public policy process, it is necessary to understand: (i) key structural and contextual dimensions, including historical, political, macroeconomic, and sociocultural issues that impact public communications and the media; (ii) key laws and institutions, including de jure/de facto legal frameworks, regulations, and institutional arrangements that impact public communication and the media; as well as (iii) key stakeholder dynamics of the actors involved in the media, including their incentives, financial resources, and human resource capacities, all of which can greatly impact the role of public communications and the media.

With these three catalytic pillars in place, this framework holds that a number of positive outcomes are possible, including better positioning by governments to ensure that public communication contributes to improved policies and services, more engaged stakeholders, and increased resilience to disinformation. In the longer term, this would help regain trust and channel these advances towards more inclusive growth.

Figure 1.1. OECD framework on public communication

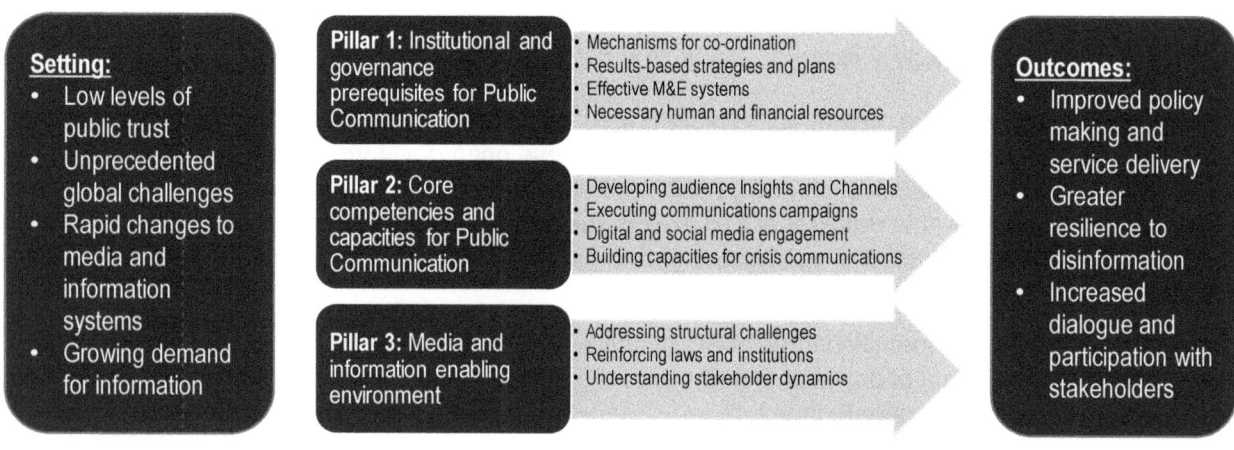

Source: Author's own work.

Summary of main findings and recommendations

Building on the analytical framework, this section offers an overview of the main findings and recommendations of the *"Citizens' Voice in Jordan: Public Communication and Media for a More Open Government"* review. It identifies actionable policy recommendations for the Government of Jordan to leverage public communication to engender a more open government, restore public trust, and move towards a more inclusive approach to policymaking. This review also analyses the opportunities to promote a sound media and information ecosystem to promote a wider variety of voices in public life.

Improving the governance of public communication in Jordan

Since 2019, Jordan embarked on an ambitious re-organisation of the public communication profession to align structures, procedures, and reporting lines within line ministries. While the Government of Jordan has achieved important progress, findings reveal room for reforms to further institutionalise and professionalise this function toward enabling a more strategic two-way communication approach. This will be all the more important as the rollout of the restructuring is exacerbating challenges in terms of operationalising new structures, facilitating co-ordination, setting an overarching strategic vision, as well as ensuring adequate human and financial resources.

Strengthening public communication structures in Jordan

Formal governance structures are a *sine qua non* condition enabling actors, processes and outcomes to foster a strategic communication centred on citizens' needs. In Jordan, the recent re-organisation process has advanced in consolidating dedicated structures at the level of line- ministries, which has repositioned this function as a key lever of government. Despite the progress to date, OECD evidence suggests that existing structures are largely uneven, and in some cases not fully functional, often lacking adequate resources, capabilities and empowerment to transition from a reactive toward a proactive communication. In this regard, efforts should continue to clarify the roles and responsibilities of media units, simplify reporting lines and facilitate intra-institutional and cross-ministerial co-ordination. Given this progress and the existing challenges, the government may consider a number of recommendations, including the following:

- Continue existing efforts to standardise and fully operationalise media units as part of the restructuring of the public communication function in Jordan, allowing for more clarity concerning their roles and responsibilities.
- Formalise communication procedures across ministries through guidelines or decrees, to ensure consistency in the role and mandate of public communicators over time and regardless of changes in leadership.
- Scaling efforts to disseminate MoSMA's manual on the organisation of media units, with an intent to expand on its content to further clarify roles and responsibilities as well as codify key communication processes.

Formalising and facilitating co-ordination mechanisms

For the successful implementation of the restructuring in Jordan, it will be critical to solidify mechanisms for vertical and inter-ministerial co-ordination among public communicators. At present, OECD evidence identifies challenges to formalising such arrangements, both across Ministries and MoSMA, as these currently remain ad hoc and informal. Nevertheless, the recent reactivation of the national network of spokespeople presents an opportunity to break siloes, optimise communication and promote good practice exchange. Its formalisation through a ministerial decree, together with the adoption of shared online tools, would not only facilitate information sharing but could also incentivise co-operation at both the strategic and technical level. Given this progress and the existing challenges, the government may consider a number of recommendations, including the following:

- Ensure the continuity of the network of communicators under the co-ordination of MoSMA to facilitate information sharing, align messages and plan join events.
- Consider formalising the network through a decree and engage in a consultation exercise with members to identify and establish a joint mandate with formal objectives, working methods, calendar of activities and digital tools and channels for engagement.
- Expand spaces for inter-ministerial dialogue on technical aspects, such as gathering of audience insights and digital communications, through the integration of new tools for information sharing and the regularisation of meetings in the framework of the network to foster the exchange of good practices.
- Consider the creation of a centralised information repository where guidelines, manuals, calendars of events and other relevant information (i.e. key campaign messages, proof points and recent policy updates) can be accessible to all public entities. This will not only support the dissemination of good practices to professionalise the work of units but also align practices.

Developing a whole-of-government communication strategy and strengthening the design, implementation, and evaluation of ministerial strategies

The Government of Jordan is gradually establishing a formal framework for public communication and media policy in the country. A set of strategies for specific media interventions were developed, including the country's first media strategy (2011-15) and the National MIL Strategy. At the level of ministries, all surveyed institutions report developing communication strategies; nevertheless, OECD evidence reveals that challenges remain in terms of establishing a whole of government vision for the public communication profession, designing quality ministerial strategies and ensuring their implementation. Given this progress and the existing challenges, the government may consider a number of recommendations, including the following:

- Develop a whole-of-government public communication strategy led by MosMA, which sets the Government's vision for reform, outlines the main objectives for its achievement and identifies concrete pillars of action and evaluation indicators to measure its success.
- Provide support for the design, implementation and evaluation of ministry-specific communication strategies. This could include the development of guidelines, the deployment of trainings and the establishment of a review committee by MoSMA to approve and evaluate sectoral strategies.
- Consider the development of a template to ensure the translation of ministerial strategies into coherent plans across all ministries.

Addressing human resource and competency gaps

At the core of professionalising public communications in Jordan is the establishment of a strategic human resource management framework ensuring adequate levels of staff and capabilities. While the ongoing restructuring seeks to align the functioning of media units, there is considerable diversity in terms of hiring practices, clarity of the mandates and skill levels. To this end, defining a core capability framework for posts could solidify gains and help consolidate a skilled workforce that is able to keep up with the rapid pace of change in the communication profession brought by new technologies and the effects of COVID-19. Given this progress and the existing challenges, the government may consider a number of recommendations, including the following:

- Develop and operationalise a dedicated competency framework for the public communication profession to provide clear entry points, requirements for advancement, and opportunities for vertical and horizontal career progression.

- Increase the professional competencies of public communicators through dedicated training programmes on topics such as audience insights, planning, messaging, digital communication, campaigns, and evaluation. An initial mapping of skill gaps could allow MoSMA to design a robust programme for the PMO, which in time could be formalised into a public skills academy or integrated into existing curricula for officials.
- Disseminate the newly created recruitment guidelines for the establishment of capabilities within media units and the promotion of professional standards.
- Recognise, award and disseminate highly-impactful communication campaigns and activities across public entities in Jordan.

Ensuring dedicated financial resources

As in many OECD countries, Jordan will need to address low levels of financial resources for the public communication profession. OECD survey results reveal that insufficient funding is the second biggest challenge on average for public communicators to carry out their key functions. With the government has made initial efforts to establish dedicated budget lines in media units, only 2 out of 14 ministries indicate these exist. Mapping future needs to allocate needed resources would help ensure the sustainability of initiatives, equip ministries with adequate tools and skills, and incentivise the regularisation of public communication practices. Given this progress and the existing challenges, the government may consider a number of recommendations, including the following:

- Establish a dedicated budget for MosMA and media units to support the deployment of core communication functions and activities. Budget allocations could be based on a mapping of funding gaps and an analysis of yearly needs based on communication plans to be developed.

Developing a more strategic use of key communication competencies in Jordan

The Government of Jordan is pursuing efforts to institutionalise internal and external communication processes and strengthen the application of core competencies. When consistently deployed, these can aid public institutions in generating buy-in around key policies, ensuring optimal flows of information, and supporting the ability of stakeholders to participate in public life. Addressing current gaps underlined by ministries to deploy campaigns, engage through digital channels, and evaluate impact will thus be critical to establishing a two-way communication.

Utilising audience insights to maximise reach and impact

Insight gathering - understood as the research into different audiences to build a knowledge base on their motivations, needs and habits – can aid in the design of more compelling and targeted government communications. Similar to several OECD countries, Jordan is taking initial steps to establish this practice. Survey data reveals that insight gathering is conducted on an occasional basis, with a small share of line ministries utilising such data to identify key messages and suitable channels. In order to leverage social listening through audience insights, the government may consider a number of recommendations, including the following:

- Ensure that the selection of key messages, channels, and visual aids respond to the needs, habits, and expectations of different segments of the population, at both the national and local level. Special attention should be given to tailoring communication for vulnerable or marginalised segments of the population, such as women, youth, and refugees among others.
- Continue the professionalisation efforts underway for the use of audience insights across ministries in Jordan by formally including it in the main mandate of the institutions of all media units and providing related training.

- Consider the creation of a central hub within the PMO to monitor, collect insights from different audiences and share it across the administration.

Leveraging the interactivity benefits of digital communication

Digital channels have become one of the primary means for the Government to communicate with the public. In this regard, most public institutions have begun consolidating an online presence through social media platforms and institutional websites. Responding to the challenges that communicators face in using online technologies, needs exist in supporting the alignment of practices, adoption of innovative digital tools, and exchange of knowledge through technical trainings and the creation of communities of practice. Additional opportunities exist for the Government of Jordan to tap into the potential of social media for a more meaningful engagement with citizens, given the wide adoption of Facebook, Twitter and YouTube by public institutions. In order to reap the benefits of digital communication, the government may consider a number of recommendations, including the following:

- Build internal capabilities to leverage the interactivity benefits of online platforms. This could take form of specialised trainings or the creation of dedicated communities of practice to share good practices on issues such as social media use, data analytics, web presence, etc.
- Ensure institutional websites and Facebook pages are up to date. Provide easy access for citizens to consult information by centralising relevant documents such as calendars of events, policy documents and other project statistics publicly.
- Communicate regularly about available consultation opportunities and make use of digital platforms, beyond just social media, to crowdsource relevant contributions from the public and establish online spaces for dialogue on key policy issues.
- Develop whole-of-government social media guidelines including for the management of institutional accounts, personal profiles of public officials and online stakeholder participation.
- Encourage collaboration with influencers, civil society and businesses to expand the scale and reach of digital communication campaigns, in particular for younger segments of the population. Such collaborations could take form of joint campaigns, with non-government stakeholders as ambassadors helping to communicate official information to different segments of society.

Evaluating the impact of public communication

Evaluating public communication is indispensable to assess the effectiveness of activities, promote accountability and build comparable evidence on what is working and what is not to inform the design of future activities. Formalising practices in this regard will be all the more important as evaluation is conducted on an ad hoc basis by two-thirds of Jordanian public institutions. Institutionalising practices and building technical skills to evaluate impact metrics, rather than outputs and outcomes, would allow for quality data to better link the contribution of communication to the Government's broader objectives. In order to best evaluate the impact of public communication, the government may consider a number of recommendations, including the following:

- Institutionalise evaluations through a whole-of-government framework with clear processes, methods, metrics, timelines, and reporting mechanisms. Such a framework could build on the impact evaluation guide from the Department of Institutional Development at the PMO and be customised to the needs of media units. Specific output, outcome and impact metrics can be identified in this framework, including for instance changes in behaviours, in levels of stakeholder participation, or in the take up of public services.
- Build technical capabilities within ministries to ground evaluations in user-driven and evidence-based approaches to inform future endeavours and policies.

- Consider the creation of a central entity in charge of overseeing the evaluation of public communication, given the highly technical nature of this task. This structure could be located within the Prime Minister's Office or another relevant institution according to the needs of the Government of Jordan.

Leveraging the media and information ecosystem in Jordan

A robust and well-regulated media and information enabling environment is vitally important to how the Government of Jordan communicates around a variety of pertinent public policy priorities. However, a number of political economy challenges exist in effectively leveraging the media and information ecosystem to support Jordan's strategic communications efforts. From a structural level, these include a growing digital divide between urban and rural areas as well as between key segments of the population. Likewise, from an institutional level, challenges include a highly complex legal framework with numerous—and sometimes overlapping—laws, directives, and regulations governing how media and broadcast organisations as well as online outlets can function. Finally, from a stakeholder level, challenges include difficulties in the accreditation of journalists, a lack of independence of certain media outlets, transparency gaps in the licencing process of key regulatory agencies, capacity challenges for government spokespeople engaging the media, as well as the changing demographics of media consumers.

Addressing structural issues affecting access to media and information

Jordan has made a significant leap in terms of advancing its digital infrastructure, media connectivity, and accessibility—including the penetration of broadband internet, cell phone technologies, and satellite access—over the past decade. However, these gains in access have not been equal across all regions of the country, pointing to the emergence of a growing digital divide on the basis of geographic and other socio-economic factors, including income, gender, and age. At the same time, exogenous or geopolitical determinants—such as the global COVID pandemic, conflicts in neighbouring countries, and an influx of refugees—are affecting how media and information is produced and consumed, especially by vulnerable groups. Given these various structural challenges, the government may consider a number of recommendations, including the following:

- Use audience insights and channel selection to target messaging and content for a wider variety of local stakeholders, which can help to bridge the digital divide to include the poor, women, and youth as key actors in the media and information ecosystem.
- Develop specialised media outreach campaigns on selected issues to specific vulnerable groups through the use of media and information literacy capacity building.

Addressing institutional issues affecting access to media and information

Jordan's constitution puts in place the necessary protections and guarantees that support freedom of expression, speech, and press, together with the 2007 law on Securing the Right to Information Access, which was the first of its kind in the Arab region. While the recent adoption of ATI protocols can support improvements to the adequacy and scope of the law, challenges remain in terms of its full-scale implementation and enforcement. In addition to these legal guarantees, a number of enabling laws, directives, and regulations govern how media and broadcast organisations as well as online outlets can function, including laws governing cybercrime, online data privacy and protection, defamation, censorship, hate speech, and secrecy; however, there is often inconsistency within this legal framework and efforts are needed to align it with international good practice. At the same time, Jordan has made notable strides in addressing mis- and dis-information, including the development of an online platform, which aims to verify the information presented in news stories and social media to prevent the spread of rumours and disinformation. To support these efforts, additional capacity building is needed to improve the practices for proactively countering mis- and dis-information, including improvements to the existing platform. Given these various institutional challenges, both formal and informal, the government may consider a number of recommendations, including the following:

- Support training and sensitisation efforts related to the recently adopted ATI protocols, which provide clear guidance on classifying, enforcing and managing information.
- Conduct a comprehensive legal review of the existing laws, regulations, and policies, with an effort to bring them into alignment with international good practices.
- Conduct an assessment of the government's efforts to counter mis- and dis-information, including a review of the "Haggak Tiraf" platform.

Stakeholder issues affecting access to media and information

Jordan has a robust media and information ecosystem with a variety of actors who produce, regulate, engage with, and consume media. Jordan's print, broadcast, radio, and online outlets are relatively diverse, and have increased over time due to liberalised laws and fewer regulatory restrictions. Despite its growth, a number of systemic challenges for news outlets in Jordan remain, including the need for greater pluralism and independence, particularly at the local levels. The journalism profession and the role of individual journalists in Jordan is largely governed by the Jordan Press Association (JPA), yet significant limitations exist in accrediting journalists working for foreign outlets as well as most other news outlets outside of the traditional print media. While Jordan has a number of regulatory institutions charged with oversight, licencing, and accreditation, challenges exist with respect to their administrative and financial independence. In addition, capacities need to be improved to better engage with journalists through the strategic use of press releases and press conferences. A final challenge is how to address the changing population demographics in order to ensure that all Jordanians benefit equally from improvements to the media enabling environment. Given these various stakeholder challenges, the government may consider a number of recommendations, including the following:

- Support an enabling environment and financial incentives –including fiscal (tax) incentives, lowering capital requirements for licencing, or providing seed-funding for local outlets—to encourage a plurality of media outlets, including those at the local levels who can better cover issues relevant to local communities.
- Support the further professionalisation of journalists through expanded accreditation procedures and local training institutions.
- Support the development of strengthening transparency and oversight mechanisms, including the development of an ombudsman or independent complaints mechanism that governs the broader media sector, including all broadcast outlets and journalists.
- Develop the capacities of government agencies that engage the media, including the institutionalisation of standardised procedures and practices, including those for press releases and press conferences.
- Support ongoing government-led Media and Information Literacy efforts to enable CSOs, citizens, and other individuals in becoming informed media consumers.

Methodology

This report analyses the contribution of the public communication function and the media ecosystem towards an open government in Jordan. It is based on a survey developed by the OECD to take stock of the existing public communication structures, policies and practices in Jordan, as well as to identify the opportunities and challenges ahead for the country to consider. In 2020, MoSMA supported the OECD with the distribution of the survey to 14 Line-Ministries in Jordan. The results submitted by MoSMA to the OECD Public Communication survey for Centres of Government (CoG) were also used as the basis of analysis for recommendations herein.

This report also builds on extensive desk research and interviews conducted with a wide variety of stakeholders during multiple fact-finding missions. A first fact-finding mission was carried out with MoSMA in 2019 to inform the findings and recommendations of this report. A workshop with the Ministries responding to the OECD survey was also conducted in September 2020 to validate the data and the main findings of this report. The report also benefitted from the input of Ms. Kristina Plavšak Krajnc, former Director of the Government Communication Office of Slovenia, in her capacity as peer reviewer. The survey was shared, discussed, and validated with the units in charge of public communication in the following public institutions in Jordan: Ministry of Transport; Ministry of Labour; Ministry of Justice; Ministry of Awqaf and Religious Affairs; Ministry of Tourism; Ministry of Entrepreneurship and Digital Economy; Ministry of Higher Education; Ministry of Education; Ministry of Trade and Industry; Ministry of Planning and International Cooperation; Ministry of Health; Ministry of Culture; Jordan Investment Commission; and the Social Security Corporation.

References

Alisal, F. (2015), *Assessment of Media Legislation in Jordan*, http://www.nyulawglobal.org/globalex/Jordan.htm. [8]

Alkhatib, W. (2017), "The Role of Media in the Arab Revolutions: Jordan", *Canadian Social Science*, Vol. 13/2, pp. 15-23, http://dx.doi.org/10.3968/9267. [10]

Freedom House (2017), *Freedom on the Net 2017 - Jordan*, https://freedomhouse.org/sites/default/files/FOTN%202017_Jordan.pdf. [13]

Government of Jordan (2018), *The National Renaissance Plan (2019-2020)*. [6]

International Republican Institute (2018), *Public Opinion Survey: Residents of Jordan*, https://www.iri.org/sites/default/files/2018.11.6_jordan_poll_presentation.pdf (accessed on 27 September 2019). [4]

Internet World Statistics (2018), *Middle East Internet Users, Population and Facebook Statistic in 2018*, https://www.internetworldstats.com/stats5.htm (accessed on 26 September 2019). [16]

Jones, D. (ed.) (2001), *Censorship: A World Encyclopedia*, Routledge. [7]

Jordan Times (2020), *Kingdom launches executive plan for media, information education*, https://www.jordantimes.com/news/local/kingdom-launches-executive-plan-media-information-education. [14]

Kardoosh, M. (2019), *Jordan struggles to reverse decades of poor economic management*, https://www.haaretz.com/opinion/.premium-jordan-struggles-to-reverse-decades-of-poor-economic-management-1.7804160. [1]

King Abdullah II ibn Al Hussein (2018), "Social or anti-social media?", *The Jordan Times*, http://www.jordantimes.com/news/local/social-or-anti-social-media (accessed on 27 September 2019). [5]

Mediterranean Network of Regulatory Authorities (n.d.), *Media Commission in Jordan*, http://www.rirm.org/en/mc-media-commission-2/ (accessed on 23 September 2019). [12]

NorthWestern University (2017), *Social Media Use in the Middle East*, http://www.mideastmedia.org/survey/2017/interactive/social-media/who-use-the-following-social-media-platforms-facebook-whatsapp-twitter-instagram-snapchat-youtube-etc.html (accessed on 26 September 2019). [17]

Northwestern University (2018), *Media Use in the Middle East*, http://www.mideastmedia.org/survey/2018/interactive/online-and-social-media/who-use-the-following-social-media-platforms.html# (accessed on 26 September 2019). [19]

OECD Development Centre (2018), *Youth Well-being Policy Review of Jordan*, EU-OECD Youth Inclusion Project, Paris, http://www.oecd.org/dev. (accessed on 26 September 2019). [18]

The Jordan Times (2019), *115 accredited media institutions in Jordan - Commission*, https://jordantimes.com/news/local/115-accredited-media-institutions-jordan-%E2%80%94-commission (accessed on 26 September 2019). [15]

UNESCO (2015), "Assessment of media development in Jordan". [9]

United Nations (2013), *Report of the Working Group on the Universal Periodic Review*, United Nations, Human Rights Council Twenty-fifth session. [11]

World Bank (2020), *Jordan Overview*, https://www.worldbank.org/en/country/jordan/overview. [3]

World Bank (2019), *Jordan's Economic Update - April 2019*, http://pubdocs.worldbank.org/en/837261553672494334/jordan-MEU-April-2019-Eng.pdf. [2]

Notes

[1] Law No. 8 of 1998, published in the Official Gazette No. 4300, p. 3162, 1 September 1998. Available in Arabic at: https://wipolex.wipo.int/en/legislation/details/11245.

[2] The Committee included the Minister of State for Media Affairs, the Minister of Awqaf and Islamic Affairs and the Minister of Culture, along with the General Secretaries of various ministries and the directors of state media institutions.

[3] The OECD understands that the Ministry of State for Media Affairs (MOSMA) is planning to develop a new national strategy for media and communications. The strategy may ultimately include areas focused on legal reforms, the media watchdog, the JPA, a media complaints commission, disinformation and community media, etc. It is not clear whether the new process has yet started nor the deadline for completion.

2 Communicating for a more open government in Jordan

This chapter seeks to provide an analytic framework to better understand the differentiated, yet complementary, roles that public communications and media ecosystems can play in supporting Open Government Reforms. As such, this chapter will discuss the current global and regional context, which underpin both the importance and timeliness of improving capacities for improved public communication and establishing the foundations for a well-functioning media and information enabling environment. Subsequently, this chapter will put forth the OECD's analytical framework, including the setting, catalysts, and potential outcomes related to improved public communication and media enabling environment. Finally, this chapter will discuss how public communication and robust media can function as complementary mechanisms for supporting Jordan's Open Government agenda as well as its COVID 19 response efforts.

Global and regional context

The last decade has witnessed a steep decline in trust in government and disengagement of citizens from public life. After sinking to a historic low of 37% in 2013, trust in government within OECD countries has only recently returned to pre-financial crisis levels of 45% only in 2019 (OECD, 2019[1]). At the same time, international observers have noted a "retreat" of democratic governance around the world. Freedom House's Freedom in the World Index (2019[2]) recorded the 13th consecutive year of decline in global freedom where, between 2005 and 2018, the share of "Not Free" countries rose to 26%, while the share of "Free" countries declined to 44%. These trends are likewise recognised by the Economist Intelligence Unit (EIU), where the 2019 Democracy Index noted the worst average global score since the index was first produced in 2006. Broadly, these poor scores were due to declining turnout in elections, decreasing trust in institutions, and diminishing civil liberties such as free speech (Economist Intelligence Unit, 2018[3]).

This challenge is particularly pertinent in the Middle East and North Africa (MENA) region, where trust in government institutions has remained low since the Arab Spring. As noted by the (2020[4]) Arab Barometer, trust in government in the region is considerably below the OECD average, including in Jordan (38%), Lebanon (19%), Morocco (29%) and Tunisia (20%). At the same time, regional instability and political turmoil, have underlined key governance challenges, which are necessary to address in rebuilding trust between the citizens and the state.

At the same time, rapid changes in the media and information sector have intensified – and sometimes helped cause – governance challenges by changing how the public consumes, communicates and shares information. These changes have affected who and what sources of information citizens trust, while the rise of social media platforms, in particular, has facilitated polarisation, as well as the spread of disinformation and of speech that promotes violence. According to the (2020[5]) Edelman Trust Barometer, 57% of respondents believe that the media is contaminated with untrustworthy information and 76% worry about false information or fake news being used as a weapon. Adding to this picture is the rise in new civic movements (e.g. climate walkouts, women's marches, protests against reduced economic opportunities, etc.), which show that citizens around the world are mobilising to demand to be heard and to participate in decision-making processes. Pre-existing challenges have been exacerbated by the COVID-19 pandemic, where capacity gaps, coupled with high levels of citizen distrust and of mis- and dis-information, are posing threats to the effectiveness of response and recovery measures.

Many OECD countries have begun to leverage open government reforms to address these critical governance challenges. In doing so, countries seek to facilitate "a culture of governance that promotes the principles of transparency, integrity, accountability and participation in support of democracy and inclusive growth (OECD, 2017[6])." However, beyond the intrinsic value of the open government principles, the implementation of related strategies and initiatives can serve as a means to improve processes and outcomes across the full spectrum of public policy. As countries around the world face the unprecedented health crisis of COVID-19, the importance of government transparency and accountability has never been more apparent (OECD, 2020[7]). In responding to the crisis, it has become ever more fundamental for citizens to be informed about government decisions and to hold politicians and policy makers to account for their actions through consistent and reliable flows of information and transparent decision-making processes.

One critical avenue to facilitate these open government principles is through the use of effective public communication and government engagement with media and information enabling environment. However, the role of public communication and the media remains under-explored as a catalyst for reinforcing the principles of transparency, integrity, accountability and stakeholder participation. Indeed, the OECD has found that in a majority of countries, communications and open government objectives are not connected overtly. For instance, while a 2017 OECD Centre of Government (CoG) survey identified the important role that CoGs attribute to public communication, data also shows that less than 10% of surveyed CoGs list promoting transparency or stakeholder participation as one of the key objectives of their communication strategy (OECD, 2017[8]). Additionally, less than 2% of Open Government Partnership action plans include commitments related to communication or the media.[1]

Nevertheless, effective public communication and resilient media are important enablers of the success of open government reforms while also reinforcing the principles of transparency, integrity, accountability, and stakeholder participation. Although MENA countries have strengthened their communication efforts and demonstrated improved competencies over the past years, this current context calls for a greater capacity and strategic deployment of communications. It is against this background that this report seeks to explore the role of communication and media as levers for more open governments, inclusive policy making, and improved service design and delivery, which can ultimately help restore trust and facilitate inclusive growth.

OECD Analytical Framework

The OECD has identified three pillars of effective public communication that can serve as policy catalysts to bring about a set of desired medium- and long-term outcomes, while building on and reinforcing open government principles (see Figure 1.1). These include:

- **Institutional and Governance Arrangements:** In order for public communication to effectively advance open government principles and serve as a tool to improve policy making and service design and delivery, it is necessary to ensure that certain institutional and governance prerequisites are in place. In particular, to ensure effective public communication across and between levels of government, it is necessary to introduce mechanisms to co-ordinate public communications functions, including horizontally (across sectors and ministries) and vertically (across levels of government). To facilitate this, results-based strategies and communications plans should be developed based on audience insights, strong M&E systems, and feedback loops to ensure an iterative approach that builds on both past success and failures alike. At the same time, a network of public communications actively engaged in the process is necessary to ensure co-ordination, exchange good practices, as well as to help professionalise the role of government communicators. Finally, the necessary human and financial resources should be in place to better support the public communications function across government.

- **Core Communications Competencies and Capacities:** In addition to having the relevant governance mechanisms in place, it is vital to ensure the development of core communication competencies with an open government focus. This includes, among others, developing audience insights and channels; executing campaigns to achieve strategic objectives; engaging digital communications, including social media; as well as building capacities for crisis communication. These competencies, when applied well, can expand the use of public communication from an information dissemination tool, to a lever of stakeholder participation, policy implementation, as well as improved service design and delivery.

- **Robust Media and Information Enabling Environment:** A final pillar to ensure effective public communication is the existence of a robust and well-functioning media and information enabling environment. To assess the potential role that media as well as the larger enabling environment can play in the public policy process, it is necessary to understand: (i) key structural and contextual dimensions, including historical, political, macroeconomic, and sociocultural issues that impact public communications and the media; (ii) key laws and institutions, including de jure/de facto legal frameworks, regulations, and institutional arrangements that impact public communication and the media; as well as (iii) key stakeholder dynamics of the actors involved in the media, including their incentives, financial resources, and human resource capacities, all of which can greatly impact the role of public communications and the media.

With these three catalytic pillars in place, this framework holds that a number of positive outcomes are possible, including better positioning by governments to ensure that public communication contributes to improved policies and services, more engaged stakeholders, and increased resilience to disinformation. In the longer term, this would help regain trust and channel these advances towards more inclusive growth (see Figure 1.1 in Chapter 1).

Role of public communication and media in the open government reform process

This section seeks to define public communication as well as what constitutes an enabling environment for the media in order to demonstrate their differentiated, yet complementary, roles in supporting policies and services, more engaged stakeholders, as well as trust in government more broadly. As will be discussed, public communications activities can equally support both: (i) internal efforts within and across the public sector as well as (ii) external initiatives to engage the public around critical policy priorities. For its part, an active and well-functioning media and information enabling environment can play an important enabling role in designing and implementing good policy design and service delivery objectives, including identifying agenda objectives, deciding among alternatives, evaluating and selecting options, implementing reforms, and monitoring and evaluating progress. With respect to the Open Government agenda more broadly, these functions can enhance government's ability to facilitate transparency, integrity, accountability, and participation—all of which create positive feedback loops to improve democratic intuitions and trust in government.

Role of public communication

Public communication is understood as "any communication activity or initiative led by public institutions for the public good," and is distinct from *political communication*, "which is linked to the political debate or to elections (OECD, 2020[9])." In the MENA region, there has been an increased recognition of the role of public communication in changing behaviours and strengthening transparency and participation. More particularly, in the context of the COVID-19 response, governments are consolidating existing crisis communication procedures, including horizontal and vertical co-ordination on communication, while progressively moving towards a more interactive use of social media. While related handbooks, guidelines, and "how-to" reports published by communications specialists from the public and private sectors have helped disseminate successful practices internationally, more efforts are needed to explore what, from a governance and public administration perspective, is needed to ensure public communications is more strategic and helps government to achieve specific policy and service delivery objectives.

From an internal perspective, public communication can support the inter-institutional dialogue, information sharing, and change management process within and across the public sector. First, it can be used to facilitate change management to ensure that public officials are aware of new public policy priorities and understand how it will affect their work. Such awareness can help to facilitate coalitions and strengthen commitment for this cause across the public sector, including among senior-level executives. Second, it can serve as a means to share knowledge—with officials becoming effective spokespeople for critical public policy priorities, including the open government agenda, within their departments and across government agencies. Finally, it can serve strategic goals, including identifying synergies between public communication officers and access to information (ATI) focal points to co-ordinate related activities horizontally and vertically across the government as well as to combat the challenges posed by mis- and dis-information.

From an external perspective, public communication can support the government's efforts to raise the awareness of citizens on key areas of government reforms, especially those aimed at enhancing transparency, integrity, accountability or stakeholder participation, and engage them in such efforts. External outreach can help with sensitisation efforts for citizens and other relevant public stakeholders so that they can better understand why certain policies have been established and what they will deliver. Citizens who are more aware of such initiatives, and who understand them better are more likely to participate in such efforts (OECD/OGP, 2019[10]). In addition, external public communication can support knowledge sharing and raise awareness among citizens of the role that they can play in supporting policies as well as the opportunities available to engage in public life. Finally, from a strategic perspective, it can seek to bring policy makers and communicators more closely together, leveraging social media and other tools to engage citizens in the policy design process to facilitate transparency and a dialogue around government initiatives.

Figure 2.1. Internal and external dimensions of public communication

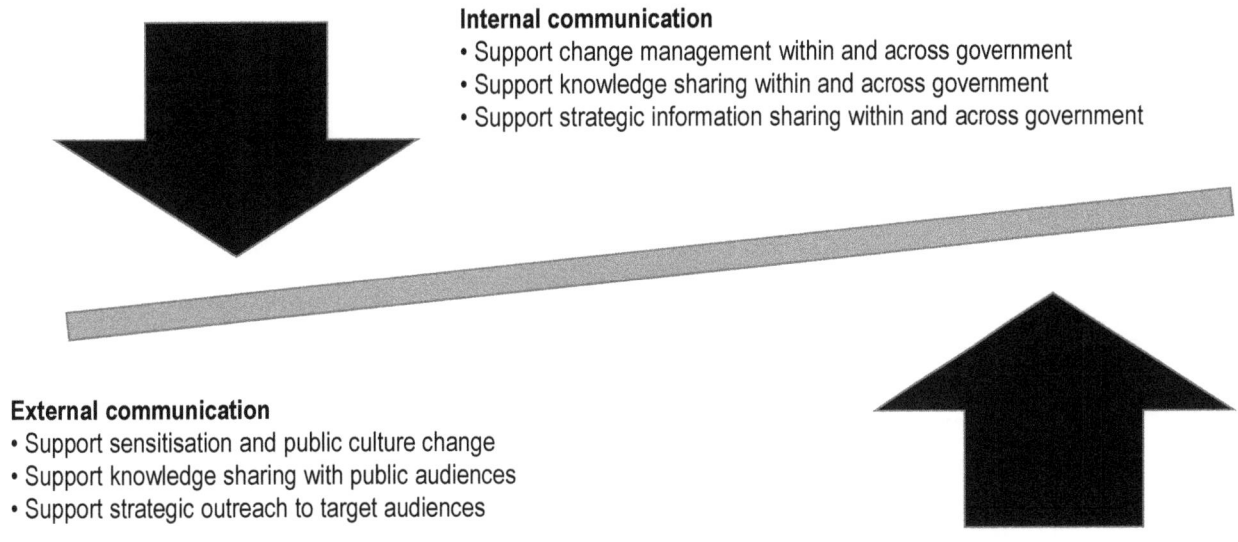

Internal communication
- Support change management within and across government
- Support knowledge sharing within and across government
- Support strategic information sharing within and across government

External communication
- Support sensitisation and public culture change
- Support knowledge sharing with public audiences
- Support strategic outreach to target audiences

Source: Author's elaboration.

Role of media and information enabling environment

The media and information enabling environment is understood as "the combination of communication, media and internet governance structures (i.e. institutional, legal, policy and regulatory frameworks) as well as principal actors (i.e. governments, traditional and social media companies and citizen journalists) that affect how the public receives and shares news and information via media platforms, government sources, and social media platforms (OECD, 2020[9])." As such, this includes the deeply interconnected roles played by traditional media actors—such as print, broadcast (e.g. radio and television)—as well as online outlets, public and private, and the journalists who work for them, both formal and informal (e.g. bloggers, activists, and citizen journalists). Likewise, it includes governmental and professional organisations that play roles in regulating, setting standards, or resolving disputes in the media sector. Finally, it includes the critical role played by media demand-side actors, such as CSOs, universities, think tanks, and research institutions—which function as key "info-mediaries"—as well as individuals, who are the end-consumers of media, whether of public interest, "info-tainment," or strictly entertainment. Taken together, these actors and institutions seek to navigate emerging challenges posed by mis- and dis-information as well as support diverse media markets, media literacy, and access to information.

In the MENA region, media and information sector play an important role in intermediating the state-citizen interface. To be sure, satellite broadcasting has created a virtual pan-Arab media space, including 34.3 million Arabic-speaking, free-to-air, satellite TV homes in the region.[2] Likewise, the use of social media over cell-phone-based platforms provides an example of how technology is enabling citizens to access information through different sources, bypassing a number of traditional hurdles (Grandvoinnet,

Aslam and Raha, 2015[11]). While domestic sources are the most important in all regions, international radio and television also hold a degree of importance, particularly in the MENA, where nearly a quarter of respondents said international TV was their most important news source (Gallup, 2015[12]).

Given the vital importance to the MENA region, the role of media and information sector can function as an arena for debate of public policies whereby different groups of society can express their ideas and opinions in a public way. Illustrating this function, Camargo and Fortunato (2015[13]) have developed a useful framework through which they seek to illustrate the influence the media can exert on public policy throughout a six stage cycle (see Figure 2.2). First, media can help to set public policy agenda and bring to bear pressure on public policy agents on issues with greater popular appeal and salience. Subsequent in the cycle, media can help to identify, evaluate, and select policy options, giving space to dispute alternatives within the media channels, foster debate of disputed options in an open and transparent manner, and allow interest groups to indicate their choices within the presented options. Finally, media can play a crucial role in implementing policies and monitoring their effects, including proving coverage of the positive and negative impacts of implemented policies and disseminating their findings to a larger public audience to evaluate (World Bank, 2016[14]).

Figure 2.2. Media and the public policy cycle

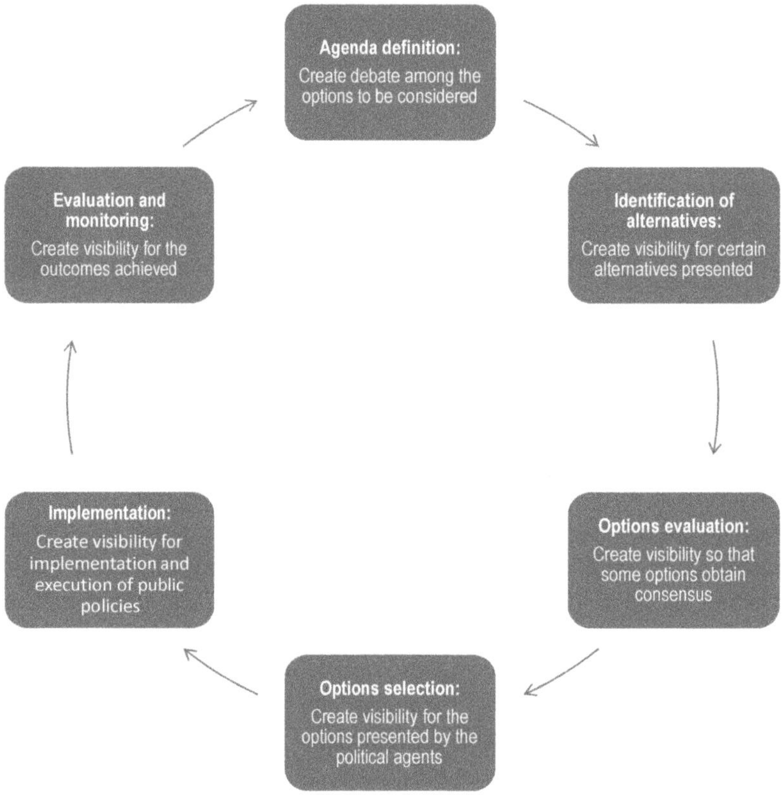

Source: Author's elaboration based on (Camargo Penteado and Fortunato, 2015[13]).

Public communication and media support for open government principles

This section examines how public communication and a media enabling environment can specifically support the principles of Open Government, including transparency, accountability, integrity, and stakeholder participation. Drawing on the existing theoretical and empirical literature, it provides evidence of how these concepts can be supported by proactive public communication, both internally and externally, as well as by a thriving media and information sector. This section also seeks to explain how these concepts link to the *OECD Recommendation of the Council on Open Government* (hereafter "the Recommendation"), the first internationally recognised legal instrument on Open Government. As demonstrated below, numerous provisions of the Recommendation provide a basis for support to improve public communications capacities as well as to support the conditions necessary for a thriving media.

Linkage with open government principles

Based on the theoretical frameworks presented above, improved public communication and a well-functioning media and information sector can greatly support Open Government principles. In particular, by developing the capacities, processes, and procedures for robust internal and external public communications, governments can ensure that information flows both from and within government in a transparent manner that informs key constituencies of key priorities and policies. Making this information available and accessible in turn lays the foundations for the application of integrity standards, the functioning of accountability institutions, and two-way feedback loops between the state and citizens. Reinforcing this process, a well-functioning media and information sector can ensure that key policy issues are called to attention and publically debated, and that the implementation of government policies are properly monitored and evaluated.

Improved transparency

Public communication, as supported by the proper strategies, plans, policies, co-ordination structures, and resources, can support transparency in a variety of manners. From an internal perspective, it can ensure that public institutions/officials are well informed about their obligations to adhere to Access to Information legislation and directives as well as Open Data policies and disclosure standards, which can facilitate the transparent flow of information related to the policies and performance of government institutions. Likewise, strong internal public communication can help to educate public institutions and officials about how to more effectively and proactively share information with "infomediaries" (e.g. CSOs, media, academia, and other institutions). From an external perspective, public communication can help to improve transparency by adequately presenting plans, policies, and reforms to the public to increase awareness of government priorities as well as communicating about Access to Information and Open Government Data for its use and re-use to improve policies and services. Finally, strong external public communication can increase the reach of such transparency initiatives by establishing the competencies and procedures for tailoring messages and using appropriate communication channels to reach different population segments.

Similarly, robust media and information enabling environment, as supported by the necessary legal, institutional, regulatory, and financial incentives, can likewise help to increase transparency. As such, the media—including the outlets and journalists developing content—can play a critical role in setting the agenda, timeline, and outcomes of planned or ongoing Access to Information or Open Government Data programmes, which are the cornerstones of enhanced government transparency. Once these and other transparency initiatives are underway, a strong media sector can help to inform citizens, CSOs, and other organisations of their rights (e.g. scope, timing, recourse, etc.) to access information about government performance vis-à-vis Access to Information as well as Open Government Data programmes. Through its investigatory and "watch-dog" role, media outlets can become key consumers of such programmes through filing Access to Information and Open Data requests as well as publicising the related information to the public on government performance. Throughout the implementation process, the media can play a critical role in evaluating and sharing the impact of such government transparency initiatives—including the reporting on government responsiveness and rejections of such requests—and making these results public.

Improved integrity

Public communication, both internal and external, can play a pivotal role in supporting the implementation of critical public sector integrity policies, including their application both within government and in society more broadly. First, from an internal perspective, it can ensure that core integrity values, principles, and standards are effectively communicated, commonly understood, and applied throughout the public sector, including those related to impartiality, honesty, conflict of interest, lobbying, and influence in policy making, open organisational culture, whistle-blower protection, ethical value statements, as well as codes of ethics or conduct. Similarly, public communication supports the effective diffusion and implementation of tailored standards developed for specific functions such as in public procurement, border and customs management, police services, as well as those for political advisors, members of government, parliament, and government suppliers.[3] Likewise, effective internal communication practices can support integrity measures, related to the use of behavioural insights,[4] education and capacity-building for integrity, adverting political capture, and ensuring transparency in the financing of political parties and electoral campaigns, as well as risk management, internal control, and audit. As such, internal public communication can assist managers in identifying an "integrity agenda" and communicating public sector values and standards within public sector organisations. From an external public communication perspective, promoting a stronger culture of integrity can be targeted through communicating public sector values externally to the private sector, civil society, and individuals, as well as supporting and nudging these partners to respect those values and standards in their interactions with public officials (OECD/OGP, 2019[10]).

As with public communication, media and information can have a large role to play with respect to integrity and anti-corruption work in countries around the world. First, the media can play a key role in bringing ideas to the table, prioritising the most pressing challenges, and putting forth solutions to improve integrity and combat corruption. Such work would include the engagement of spokespeople from "watchdog" organisations, citizens groups, labour unions, and independent media. If and when the case allows, media can suggest and foster debate across the most pertinent topics related to integrity and anti-corruption, including among others, legislation on conflicts of interest, lobbying and political finance, public procurement, internal control and audit, as well as whistle-blower protections. In a subsequent step, the media can help foster debate to evaluate the applicability and necessity of additional integrity and anti-corruption measures, determine which measures are most relevant, and pressure policy makers to adopt key measures in the public discourse. Finally, the media has a great opportunity to oversee the implementation, monitoring, and reporting on the effectiveness of existing integrity and anti-corruption measures. As such, reporting on the *de facto* implementation of existing legislation can provide a critical means to ensure improved integrity, reduced corruption, and more robust rule of law.

Improved accountability

Public communication has an essential role to play in reinforcing accountability relationships, processes, and institutions. From an internal perspective, it can support the mandates of government accountability institutions, including the Office Auditor General, Supreme Audit Intuition, Ombudsman's office, or other related institutional mechanism. In doing so, it can inform public sector employees about the various venues and mechanisms to ensure that government performance is supervised in a manner to ensure both effectiveness and efficiency. From an external perspective, it can likewise support demand-side actors in accessing and interfacing with accountability institutions, both formal and informal, as well as the public information necessary for CSOs to adequately monitor government performance. With respect to the former, this would include informing citizens of the existing oversight and control institutions, mechanisms, and processes, including the role of the Ombudsman's office, the supreme audit institution, and other Grievance Redress Mechanisms (GRMs). With respect to the latter, this would include informing citizens of existing social accountability mechanisms, including citizen report cards, social audits, participatory budgeting, etc.

Likewise, a robust media and information enabling environment can ensure that accountability mechanisms and processes are applied in a fair and equitable manner in accordance with law. As such, media can play a key role in setting and maintaining the public policy agenda to focus on both horizontal and vertical accountability measures that are in place. This includes following and reporting on the findings of Supreme Audit Institutions, Legislative oversight committees, and Ombudsman's office on issues of public importance. Likewise, this could include publicity and advocacy for vertical accountability institutions, including informing the public what social accountability mechanisms exist for citizens, CSOs, and other organisations as well as what other good practices exist in other countries. Finally, the media can play a role in monitoring the use of existing social accountability mechanisms, evaluating their impacts, and using their findings to hold public officials to account.

Improved stakeholder participation

Finally, public communication has an essential role in ensuring the effective interface between the state and citizen, including the establishment of two-way engagement mechanisms. Internally, it is necessary to sensitise public sector employees of the existing laws and directives related to stakeholder participation, which may vary across departments, ministries, and agencies. Equally important, internal public communication needs to ensure that the proper guidelines, standards, and procedures are disseminated to public officials in conducting these consultations. This can involve the types of mechanisms used, the statutory period allowed for review and comment, and the standards related to follow-up and reporting. Externally, public communication's role is even larger in ensuring effective stakeholder participation. As such, an effective campaign or strategy would involve, *inter alia*: (i) informing the public about the existence of participatory mechanisms and digital platforms for dialogue; (ii) mobilising stakeholders to partake in consultations and innovative citizen participation practices; (iii) providing stakeholders with the necessary information to contribute to public decision making; (iv) establishing sanctioned fora for the public (e.g. CSO, citizens, private sector) to express their opinions; and (v) providing information on how public consultations were recorded and followed-up on. All of these efforts should be undertaken with a view to reach different segments of the population—including marginalised and under-represented groups—to broaden the scope of participating stakeholders, beyond those traditionally in possession of access and influence.

Finally, media and information can help to facilitate stakeholder participation practices across levels of government. First, media can provide information and publicise existing participation mechanisms, as well as ongoing consultation processes where the government is seeking feedback from citizens, CSOs, and other organisations. In this regard, the media can help to present the public with different options, highlight the merits of each, and provide recommendations and endorsements. Similarly, the media can play a watch-dog role whereby it can shine a spotlight on government decisions and processes that did not properly follow participation guidelines or allow adequate time for comment. Finally, the media can monitor and evaluate the impact of participatory processes, including reporting on how consultations were eventually incorporated into news laws and policies.

Linkage with the OECD Recommendation on open government

In December 2017, the OECD Council adopted the Recommendation, the first internationally recognised legal instrument on Open Government. Its adoption originated in more than 15 years of evidence-based analysis of Open Government strategies and initiatives, the OECD's Report on *Open Government: The Global Context and the Way Forward* (2016[15])as well as a successful online public consultation. The Recommendation provides the substantive framework for all the work the OECD implements in this policy area and guides the work of the OECD Working Party on Open Government, which brings together OECD member and partner countries to discuss how to further advance open government reforms (OECD, 2017[6]). In this context, the OECD has recognised public communication and the media as a key tool for promoting open government, and included it in several provisions of its Recommendation (see Figure 2.3):

- **Provision 6 of the Recommendation** reinforces the need to "actively communicate on open government strategies and initiatives, as well as on their outputs, outcomes and impacts, in order to ensure that they are well-known within and outside government, to favour their uptake, as well as to stimulate stakeholder buy-in" (OECD, 2017[6]). Accordingly, Provision 6 encourages countries to actively communicate about related strategies and initiatives, so that they are known by the larger public and not just a select group of civil society actors or engaged citizens. In maximising public communications, both internally and externally, a flourishing media can help by advancing the Open government agenda, developing and advocating new initiatives, and informing stakeholders about the current policies and ongoing reforms.

- **Provision 7 of the Recommendation** reinforces the need to "proactively make available clear, complete, timely, reliable and relevant public sector data and information that is free of cost, available in an open and non-proprietary machine-readable format, easy to find, understand, use and reuse, and disseminated through a multi-channel approach, to be prioritised in consultation with stakeholders" (OECD, 2017[6]). Accordingly, Provision 7 underlines the importance of communicating about public sector data and information and making it easily available to stakeholders in a clear, complete, timely and reliable manner. The media can likewise amplify this role by publicising Access to Information websites, Open Data portals, and other public transparency efforts. As a public "watchdog" the media can also play a key role in filing ATI and Open Data requests, using this information to develop politically salient messaging for target audiences, and reporting where information requests have been refused.

- **Provision 8 of the Recommendation** reinforces the need to "grant all stakeholders equal and fair opportunities to be informed and consulted and actively engage them in all phases of the policy-cycle and service design and delivery" (OECD, 2017[6]). This should be done with adequate time and at minimal cost, while avoiding duplication to minimise consultation fatigue. Further, specific efforts should be dedicated to reaching out to the most relevant, vulnerable, underrepresented, or marginalised groups in society, while avoiding undue influence and policy capture." Accordingly, providing feedback to stakeholders on the outcomes of the participation process is at the core of the definition of "consultation," and this requires effective public communication, both internally and externally. In this regard, the media can likewise highlight to public audiences key policy initiatives from which the government is currently soliciting feedback, monitoring the feedback process, and reporting how public consultations were eventually incorporated into the law.

- **Provision 10 of the Recommendation** reinforces the need to "explore the potential of moving from the concept of open government toward that of open state" (OECD, 2017[6]). Accordingly, as part of Provision 10 on open state, the Recommendation recognises the role of other non-governmental actors, including that of media, to support relevant initiatives. Importantly, the media can assist with the Open State agenda by supporting agenda definition, debating on policy options, supervising, implementing, and reporting on results at the local level as well as across different branches of government, including the legislature and judiciary.

Figure 2.3. Public communication provisions of the OECD Recommendation on open government

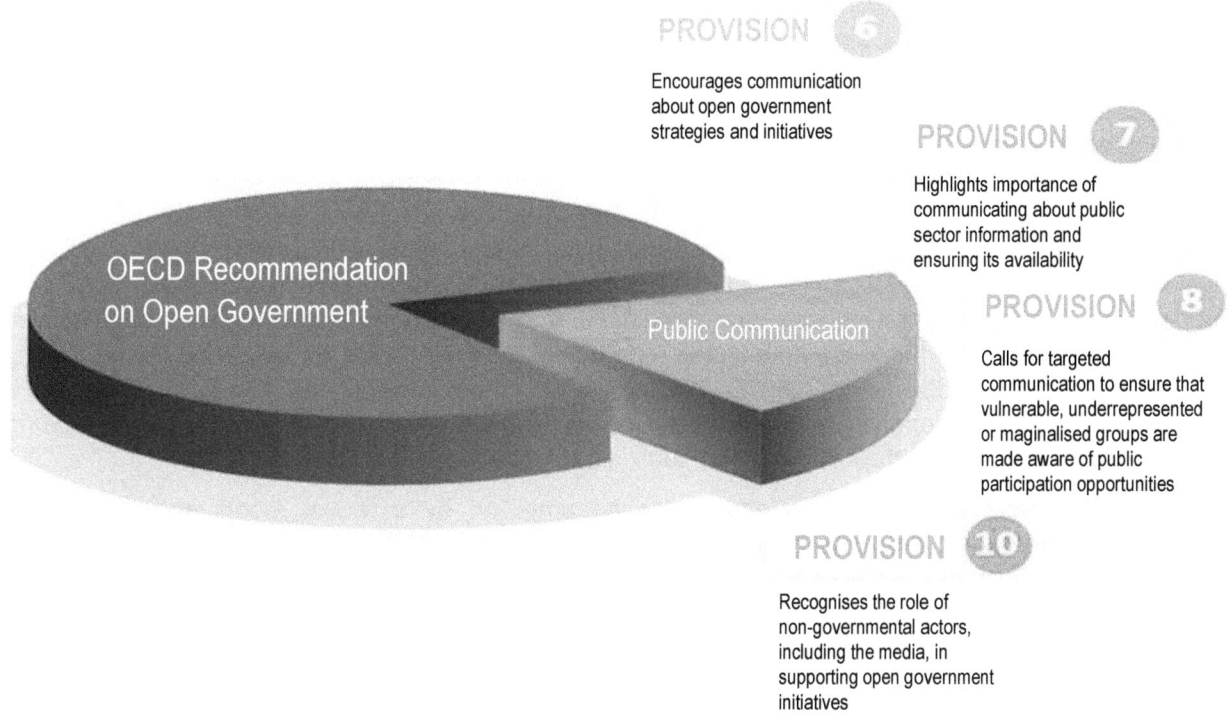

Source: Based on the OECD 2020 Analytical Framework, internal document.

Communicating for an open government in Jordan

This section seeks to link the aforementioned benefits of public communication and a robust media enabling environment with ongoing government public communication efforts around key issues, including the COVID-19 response as well as Open Government reforms in Jordan, among others. In particular, this section seeks to provide a range of options for applying both internal and external public communication activities to these and other public policy areas. Likewise, this section will link the benefits of a well-functioning media and information sector in order to demonstrate how these messaging efforts can be supported and amplified in Jordan. Finally, this section will show how both public communications and an enabling media and information environment can support improved transparency, integrity, accountability, and participation.

Public communication and media in the COVID-19 response

In responding to the crisis, it has become even more fundamental for citizens to be informed about government decisions and to hold politicians and policy makers to account for their actions through consistent and reliable flows of information and transparent decision-making processes. Similar to many countries in the world, the COVID-19 crisis in Jordan has put pressure on the government and public administration to respond quickly to ensure the health and safety of citizens. In line with the country's overarching principle, "prioritise human safety," the government has mobilised a massive amount of resources to confront the pandemic head on, "investing in affordable and widespread testing, delivering food and necessary items to households, and lowering sales tax on key protective equipment," according to the Minister of Finance (IMF, 2020[16]). At the same time, the Social Security Investment Fund has also enacted a wide set of policies, including in-kind transfers and benefits for the unemployed and self-employed (Ibid).

Given both these challenges and the government's response to the pandemic thus far, it is clear that public communication has a crucial role to play in the crisis response. From an internal perspective, public communications can help support knowledge sharing, the dissemination of strategic information, and change management practices within and across government in an effort to help design and deploy the most effective and responsive policies to counter the current crisis. Moreover, effective public communication by the centre of government is key in this pandemic to "ensure coherence of government messaging internally, so that various ministers, department, and agencies are able to respond with one voice as well as to pre and debunk mis- and dis-information" (OECD, 2020[7]). From an external perspective, public communication around the crisis responses can support sensitisation to new policies, knowledge sharing with public audiences around new policy measures, as well as to strategically engage vulnerable populates. The OECD has noted that behavioural communication campaigns have played an important role in facilitating the enforcement of regulations, by "nudging or instructing wide segments of the population to comply with required measures – from washing their hands, to respecting the provisions of lockdowns and social distancing" (OECD, 2020[7]). Public communication can also be mobilised as a key means to fight disinformation, which can "reduce compliance with the emergency measures being enacted, thereby threatening their efficacy and public trust in the response" (OECD, 2020[17]).

Likewise, such public communication efforts can be amplified by a robust media and information environment, especially in response to a quickly changing operating environment. As noted above, an effective media and information environment can help to set the public policy agenda; identify, evaluate, and select policy options; as well as to monitor the effects of policies that have been implemented. All of these functions are critically relevant to the COVID-19 response, especially as governments grapple with "large amounts of changing information, pressures to respond in a more effective and efficient manner, and face a surge in disinformation" (OECD, 2020[7]). Across the MENA region, countries have already begun to implement media outreach measures such as campaigns on TV, radio and social media to raise awareness among citizens about hygiene rules and preventive measures to curb the spread of COVID-19 (OECD, 2020[18]). Likewise, governments also developed websites and used social media to respond to the most frequently asked questions, to avoid misinformation, and to provide tips to help prevent the spread of this pandemic (ibid).

Supporting Jordan's open government reforms

In addition to responding to the most immediate public policy areas, including responding to the COVID-19 pandemic, the role of public communication and a robust media and information sector can help to promote long-term public policy objectives that support government transparency, integrity, accountability, and stakeholder participation. Indeed, many of these are included as part of Jordan's National Renaissance Plan (2019-20),[5] which puts forth a vision for transformation based on combatting corruption and enhancing transparency and integrity as critical factors to strengthen institutions. Similar principles are captured by Jordan's commitments to the Open Government Partnership (OGP), which it joined in 2011 as the first Arab country in the initiative. To date, Jordan has submitted four national actions plans, and it is currently conducting a consultation to finalise its 5th National Action Plan, which promises to be the most ambitious, focused and participative to date. In this regard, Jordan is currently implementing 5 commitments from its 4th NAP (2018-20), for which public communications and the media can provide a great deal of support during the final implementation phase. These include the following:

- Enhancing partnership and dialogue between the public sector and Civil Society.
- Development and enhancement of the application of Government Open Data Policy.
- Fostering national dialogue to achieve political reform.
- Unification and development of the national Human Rights violations' complaints mechanism.
- Institutionalisation of the enforcement measures for the Access to Information Law.

Given the priorities enshrined by the National Renaissance plan as well as the 4th OGP National Action Plan, as well as the Indicative Executive Program (2021–2023) and the forthcoming Government Economic Recovery Priorities Plan, there is a great role that public communication can play in implementing these initiatives as well as supporting the larger principles behind them. For instance, from an internal perspective, public communication supports broader change management objectives within government to instil Open Government principles across the workstreams and professional competencies of various ministries, departments, and agencies. Similarly, internal communication can help to share knowledge about Open Government Partnership (OGP) reform objectives across government departments as well as to share strategic information, which can help contribute to the achievement of the 4th NAP priorities, many of which are cross-cutting and involve work by multiple government entities. From an external perspective, public communication can help support these key initiatives—namely the National Renaissance Plan and the 4th OGP NAP—by sensitising key audiences and emphasising the benefits of these reform areas. This can be done through public information campaigns, media and information literacy trainings, as well as by gathering audience insights to effectively target key audiences. By informing citizens of these and other on-going public policies, public communicators can increase buy-in and support for these reforms as well as better understand citizen needs in the reform process.

Likewise, the success of Jordan's transparency, integrity, accountability and participation reforms depends on a robust and active media. In this regard, the media can play an important role in setting the policy agenda as part of the consultation process for future OPG National Action Plans in Jordan. As such, they can play a key role in publicising and reporting on the outcomes of the various National Dialogues, which are held around key Open Government themes. Likewise, the media play an essential role in the eventual selection of new Open Government initiatives by their ability to foster debate and dialogue around the benefits and consequences of such policies. Finally, as part of its "watchdog" functions, media can help to monitor the implementation of ongoing Open Government reforms, and highlight areas for improvement.

References

Arab Barometer (2020), *Arab Barometer Survey*, https://www.arabbarometer.org/survey-data/. [4]

Camargo Penteado, C. and I. Fortunato (2015), "Mídia e políticas públicas: possíveis campos exploratórios", *Revista Brasileira de Ciências Sociais*, Vol. 30/87, p. 129, http://dx.doi.org/10.17666/308705-17/2015.129-141. [13]

Economist Intelligence Unit (2018), *Democracy Index 2017: Free speech under attack*, http://pages.eiu.com/rs/753-RIQ-438/images/Democracy_Index_2017.pdf. [3]

Edelman (2020), *2020 Edelman Trust Barometer*, https://www.edelman.com/trust/2020-trust-barometer. [5]

Freedom House (2019), *Freedom in the World 2019 Scores*, https://freedomhouse.org/report/freedom-world/2019/scores. [2]

Gallup (2015), *Gallup World Poll 2015: Most Important Media that Citizens Report Using for News by Region*. [12]

Grandvoinnet, H., G. Aslam and S. Raha (2015), *Opening the Black Box: The Contextual Drivers of Social Accountability*, The World Bank, http://dx.doi.org/10.1596/978-1-4648-0481-6. [11]

IMF (2020), *Inside Jordan's Fight to Tackle COVID-19*, https://www.imf.org/en/News/Articles/2020/07/16/na071620-inside-jordans-fight-to-tackle-covid19. [16]

OECD (2020), "Combatting COVID-19 disinformation on online platforms", *OECD Policy Responses to Coronavirus (COVID-19)*, OECD Publishing, Paris, https://dx.doi.org/10.1787/d854ec48-en. [17]

OECD (2020), "COVID-19 crisis response in MENA countries", *OECD Policy Responses to Coronavirus (COVID-19)*, OECD Publishing, Paris, https://dx.doi.org/10.1787/4b366396-en. [18]

OECD (2020), *OECD Centre of Government Survey 2020: Understanding Public Communication*. [9]

OECD (2020), "Transparency, communication and trust: The role of public communication in responding to the wave of disinformation about the new Coronavirus", *OECD Policy Responses to Coronavirus (COVID-19)*, OECD Publishing, Paris, https://dx.doi.org/10.1787/bef7ad6e-en. [7]

OECD (2019), *Government at a Glance 2019*, OECD Publishing, Paris, https://dx.doi.org/10.1787/8ccf5c38-en. [1]

OECD (2017), *Organisation and functions at the centre of government: Centre Stage II*. [8]

OECD (2017), "Recommendation of the Council on Open Government", *OECD Legal Instruments*, OECD-LEGAL-0438, OECD, Paris, https://legalinstruments.oecd.org/en/instruments/OECD-LEGAL-0438. [6]

OECD (2016), *Open Government: The Global Context and the Way Forward*, OECD Publishing, Paris, https://dx.doi.org/10.1787/9789264268104-en. [15]

OECD/OGP (2019), *Communicating Open Government: A How-To Guide*, Open Government Partnership, https://www.opengovpartnership.org/documents/communicating-open-government-a-how-to-guide-oecd-ogp/. [10]

World Bank (2016), *Making Politics Work for Development: Harnessing Transparency and Citizen Engagement*, Washington, DC, http://dx.doi.org/10.1596/978-1-4648-0771-8. [14]

Notes

[1] Author's own research, conducted in January 2019 through the OGP database.

[2] Digital TV Research on the Middle East and North Africa (2015).

[3] OECD, "Standards", OECD Public Integrity Handbook, 2020.

[4] For instance, this is used to define core integrity standards and values, to ensure select values and principles are actually fit for purpose in a given county.

[5] Jordan Renaissance Plan (2019-20), https://your.gov.jo/.

3 Improving the governance of public communication in Jordan

This chapter will analyse the actors, structures and processes underpinning the public communication model in Jordan. In doing so, it looks at how the government of Jordan can effectively strengthen related institutional arrangements, formalise co-ordination mechanisms across levels of government, develop a whole-of-government communication strategy, as well as address human and financial resource gaps. It will discuss the building blocks of a whole-of-government communication approach and provide guidance for a more strategic deployment of this function by MoSMA and line ministries. Finally, it will identify recommendations to support the current re-organisation of the communication function in the country.

Introduction

Since 2019, Jordan embarked on an ambitious re-organisation of the public communication function across government to align structures, procedures, and reporting lines. In pursuit of the priorities outlined in 2019-20, the Government notably issued an official directive for the administrative reform of media units within ministries. These reforms can help further position public communication as a key enabler of government, and support the country's transition toward a more strategic use of this function to promote better policies and services. Ultimately, a communication approach grounded in the open government principles of transparency and participation can aid in the implementation of ongoing reforms, strengthen trust and support the attainment of key policy objectives.

The ongoing restructuring in Jordan can be better understood when analysed against two common governance models for public communication – namely tactical and strategic. This distinction draws from existing literature underlining the multi-layered and organisationally diverse nature of this function across the world (Sanders and Canel, 2013[1]; Gelders and Ihlen, 2010[2]; Luoma-aho and Canel, 2020[3]). Notably, the framework is characterised by a set of elements defining the degree to which structures, processes and resources are institutionalised on the one hand, and professionalised on the other (see Table 3.1). In practice, public communication archetypes within a given country are made up of a mix of the below elements ranging from the purely tactical to the highly strategic, with varying transitions between categories.

Table 3.1. Features of tactical and strategic governance models of public communication

Features range from tactical (left) to strategic (right)

	Tactical	Transitional	Strategic
Public Communication Structures	• Staff covers communication activities irregularly and alongside other functions • Only a press officer is in charge of all communication aspects • Limited authority and/or contact with decision makers	• A communication professional manages all activities • Some access and buy-in from decision makers	• Dedicated unit with specialised and trained personnel • Unit represented at decision makers level
Co-ordination Mechanisms	• Communication is conducted in silos, without awareness of activities in other government agencies • There are no common practices nor standards • Messages on core subjects vary between departments, or are not respected • There can be overlap in the work of different offices	• There is some co-ordination from the CoG or another entity, perhaps covering only some areas of communication or specific projects • Some key messages are agreed and mostly used consistently • Some steps are taken to harmonise the visual identity of the government.	• Processes and protocols are clear and abided by, and create efficiencies • There is high message discipline • Time-intensive tasks (e.g. monitoring) are centralised within a dedicated entity
Formalisation of communication strategic approaches	• Communications follow events without advance planning • Objectives of communication activities or strategies are not agreed upon in writing • Activities and channels of communication are not differentiated by audiences	• Some overarching objectives are stated and elaborated into a strategy, but parts of communication activity remain ad hoc and unrelated to them • Some communication follow pre-defined plans • Simple audience insights • Some communication are tailored to specific audiences (e.g. youth, women)	• Communication priorities are agreed in consultation with policy makers and other relevant stakeholders and are driven by stated objectives that align with the organisation's goals • Short-term planning is managed through a forward-planning grid • Strategies informed by audience insights and monitoring and evaluation • Implementation of pre-defined plans

Human resources and competencies	• Communication staff are appointed by political figures and change with each election or change at the top • Staff lacks specialised background and/or training. • No clearly defined job descriptions.	• Staff includes both political appointees and civil servants • Staff receive basic training or have previous relevant experience	• Civil servants are in charge of public communication, which are kept separate from political communication • Staff is highly professionalised and regularly trained to stay abreast of innovation • New functions and/or new departments are created to modernise communication
Financial resources	• No dedicated budget is available and/or financing for communication staff and activities is volatile. • Lack of budget efficiency	• Budget is shared with another function or is ad hoc • A dedicated budget exists but does not match the communication objectives/ is insufficient	• A dedicated budget guarantees continued delivery against objectives • Financial resources can be allocated for larger activities according to priorities • Financial transparency and performance accountability to maximise budget efficiency

Source: Author's own work, based on (Sanders and Canel, 2013[1]).

On the one side of the spectrum, a tactical model of communication relies on one-way information sharing measures for the attainment of short- to medium-term objectives. These types of communication are often ad hoc and fragmented due to weak structures, capacities and resources across public institutions. Consequently, communication under this model is primarily of a reactive nature and serves an auxiliary role at best.

In contrast, a strategic model offers the greatest potential for governments to ensure communication is an instrument of policy making and a means to engage with citizens on issues that matter most to them. Communication initiatives follow formal strategies, structures, guidelines and processes, which respond to the attainment of long-term policy goals. They are user-driven in nature and employ sophisticated tools and methods delivered through a well-resourced office with a strong leadership and mandate.

To pursue the objectives outlined in a host of Government plans,[1] including the Indicative Executive Program (2021-2023) and the forthcoming Government Economic Recovery Priorities Plan, Jordan will need to continue its reforms toward a more strategic operating model for public communication. In this regard, the public communication restructuring efforts offer a valuable opportunity to develop the capacity of staff to engage in two-way exchanges with citizens and to leverage related activities to improve policies and services.

Strengthening public communication structures in Jordan

This section will explore the current institutional arrangements governing this important function in Jordan. The analysis will be based on data collected on the mandates, composition, appointment and functioning of organisational structures. Despite the progress and reforms to date, OECD evidence suggests that existing structures are largely uneven and, where they are in place, often lack adequate resources, capabilities and empowerment to transition from the tactical to the strategic spectrum. The ongoing restructuring led by MoSMA, however, provides a timely opportunity to address these concerns by clarifying roles and responsibilities, aligning mandates, establishing clear accountability lines and standardising procedures.

The organisation of the public communication function varies significantly across OECD countries in terms of the degree of centralisation and formality (OECD, 2021[4]). This can take the form of a single institution steering communication across government or a devolved model where each institution has its independent mandate. For example, public communication in Australia is a shared responsibility across multiple government agencies, whereas in the United Kingdom this is led by a unit at the CoG[2] (see Box 3.1).

> **Box 3.1. Examples of public communication structures in OECD countries**
>
> **The Government Communication Service (GCS) in the United Kingdom**
>
> The Government Communication Service (GCS) is a professional body composed of over 4 500 communication professionals supporting and promoting the work of 25 ministerial departments, 21 non-ministerial departments and over 300 agencies and other public bodies. The aim of this entity is to deliver "world-class public service communications that support government priorities, enable the efficient and effective operation of public services and improve people's lives".
>
> GCS acts as a central government communication node and is considered as one of 14 functions that operate across the civil service. The entity was created to support communication professionals employed in central government departments, agencies and arm's length bodies to professionalise public communication through its core values of integrity, honesty, objectivity and impartiality.
>
> **The Communications Advice Branch in Australia**
>
> Whole-of-government communication is a shared responsibility across multiple government agencies and different officers responsible for supporting the work of the executive government (e.g. ministerial media advisers, press secretaries, etc.). For instance, the Communications Advice Branch within the Department of Finance provides specialist advice to non-corporate Commonwealth entities undertaking advertising campaigns; advises the relevant ministers on the framework for campaigns; and manages the Campaign Advertising Supplier Register.
>
> Source: Based on the responses to the Centre of Government Public Communication survey for the *OECD Report on Public Communication: The Global Context and the Way Forward* (OECD, 2021[4]).

While there is no single best arrangement, there are common elements supporting the effective functioning of these structures. First, consistency of communication mandates across government that are in written form and set clear roles and responsibilities are important factors ensuring their legitimacy (IFAC and CIPFA, 2014[5]). Second, the empowerment of all communicators within the organisation—together with clear accountability lines, objectives, and the monitoring of performance—are key to ensure the effectiveness of operations (Luoma-aho and Canel, 2020[3]). Third, the establishment of core professional values directing the work of public communicators under a common approach and detaching it from political priorities, in addition to grounding activities in the open government principles of transparency, integrity, accountability, and stakeholder participation. These elements, together with adequate human and financial resources, are critical to the effectiveness of communication structures.

At the centre-of-government level in Jordan, public communication is steered by MoSMA within the Prime Minister's Office (PMO). According to OECD survey responses, this unit is primarily responsible for communicating government decisions, actions and results. It also oversees public communication policy, conducts internal communication in the PMO, as well as co-ordinates activities with other public authorities. The Minister officially covers the function of government spokesperson and shares official announcements. Other functions that MoSMA carries out include the development of media campaigns, the gathering of insights, engagement with the media, as well as the deployment of digital and crisis communication.[3] To carry out these functions, the unit is composed of approximately 22 individuals working full-time.[4] Staff within MosMA also often provide support to other government entities upon request.

While MoSMA has achieved progress in consolidating a central public communication hub in Jordan, several challenges need to be addressed to ensure the effectiveness and impact of its current work. To this end, it will be critical to guarantee adequate levels of staff, resources, and training to ensure MoSMA's capacity to deliver as the leading structure. Interviews with stakeholders also revealed that PMO staff often have to operate on a reactive basis given the high levels of demand for their support. Formalising existing procedures in a framework or guidance document, as well as developing a dedicated strategy, may support the consolidation of existing good practices within the institution.

At the level of ministries, the recent re-organisation process successfully achieved the creation of dedicated structures to communicate between the Jordanian state and citizens. These efforts are an important step in consolidating a professional public communication service and signal the recognition attributed to this function in the country. Public officials during OECD interviews underlined that further efforts and resources are needed to ensure the effective operation of such structures, as institutional arrangements are newly established or not yet fully functional.

Figure 3.1. Types of communication structures in Jordanian ministries

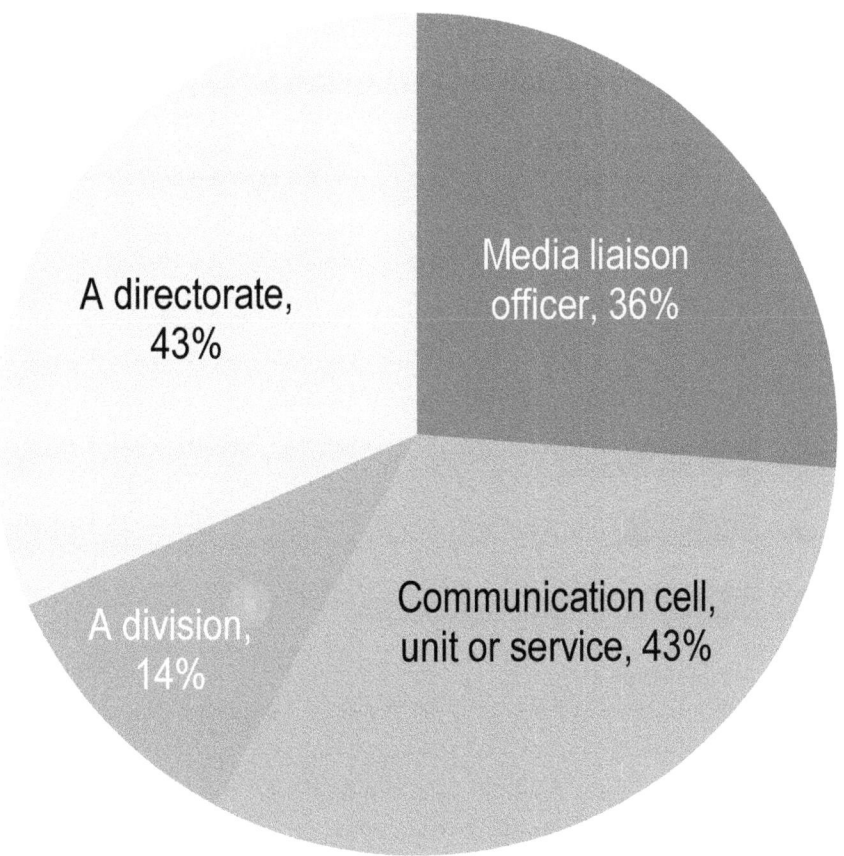

Note: N=14. Options for this question were not mutually exclusive. 3 out of 5 ministries that selected "Media Liaison Officers" also selected unit, division or directorate. 5 ministries selected 2 options respectively.
Source: OECD (2020), Survey for line-ministries in Jordan: Understanding public communication in Jordan.

Indeed, OECD findings suggest that communication structures in Jordan tend to vary significantly in terms of their organisation, functioning, and level of resources. As Figure 3.1 illustrates, a large majority of them take the form of a unit (43%), directorate (43%) or division (14%) with the support of media liaison officers. In addition to these institutional arrangements, OECD fact-finding interviews indicated that press officers exist and are tasked with reporting key information, in particular around cabinet decisions. Nonetheless, a small share of ministries (2 out of 14) rely on the work of a single individual, which signals the uneven levels of capacities and resources available across institutions. Findings from an OECD validation workshop echoed this duality, where in some cases complex structures exist with several departments for media, public relations, and communication.

Factors such as decision-making processes, appointments, reporting lines and specific sector needs may explain differences in terms of the composition and operation of these structures. As Figure 3.2 illustrates, data suggests that most staff with communication responsibilities are civil servants (as opposed to political appointees for example). Nonetheless, interviews with stakeholders revealed that the effectiveness of such teams rely on factors such as individual effort, personality of staff, leadership in place as well as available resources. An additional challenging aspect that was underscored was the burdensome reporting lines and often-bureaucratic procedures that need to be followed, which at times hinder the impact and speed of initiatives and de-incentivises co-ordination. Such arrangements differ from entities where communication staff have a direct means of interaction with the Minister while others need to navigate several layers of approval before being able to disseminate information. All of the elements discussed herein have implications on the ability of staff to separate political from public communication.

Figure 3.2. Types of appointments in Jordanian line ministries

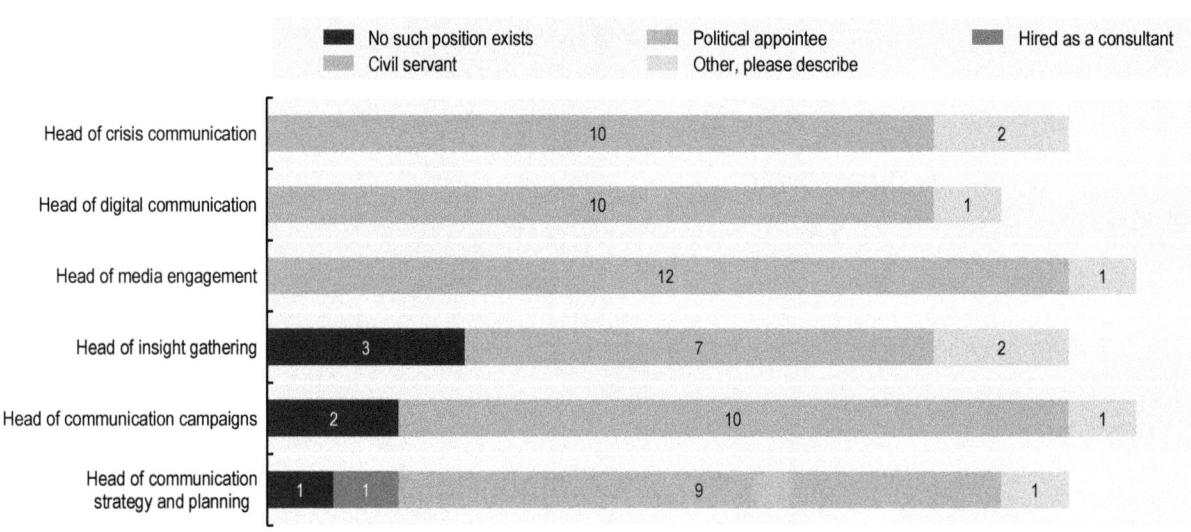

Note: N=14. The graph depicts number of ministries.
Source: OECD (2020), Survey for line-ministries in Jordan: Understanding public communication in Jordan.

Broadly, differing structures that are not institutionalised make it difficult to carry out public communication with a strategic perspective. Findings from an OECD validation workshop note that different institutional arrangements exacerbate administrative challenges facing the work of media units, through unclear roles and responsibilities, burdensome reporting lines, and a difficulty to separate the political and public agendas. This is all the more challenging as the roles and empowerment of communicators are subject to change with a new government. Findings also revealed that the lack of institutionalisation is sometimes leading to different mandates with diverging objectives and practices that ultimately result in misaligned messaging to the public.

For the ongoing restructuring to be effective, efforts must continue to clarify the roles and responsibilities of media units, simplify reporting lines and facilitate intra-institutional and cross-ministerial co-ordination. Together with the modernisation of capabilities through trainings, this could help institutionalise procedures and set professional communication standards. As part of the restructuring process, MoSMA has also developed a manual for media units to align their organisation and functioning. It is intended to "define the basic tasks and roles of these units" in order to work on "strengthening the role of media actors to support the government in communicating its messages and explaining its policies to the public" (Almalakatv,

2020[6]). Efforts should focus on its ample dissemination and implementation to standardise procedures, clarify roles, and promote a more co-ordinated approach across government. This is a practice adopted by several OECD and partner countries (see Box 3.2).

Box 3.2. Examples of manuals and guidelines for public communicators in OECD member and partner countries

Finland's Central Government Communication Guidelines

The Government of Finland developed a series of guidelines, recognising freedom of speech, openness and impartiality as core values of the administration. The fifth edition of the Guidelines explains the values governing communication, outlines the duties and describes the changes in the field of communication and how these changes impact public authorities. It serves as a basis for government organisations to draw up their own more detailed communication guidelines.

Costa Rica's Government Communication Manual

The Ministry of Communications in Cost Rica developed a manual on government communication to support the implementation of the country's strategy and objectives. It sets out the main elements of the whole-of-government narrative and messaging, which is updated on a yearly basis. It also includes a series of principles in regard to editorial work, digital communication, graphic and audio-visual content, and the use of text messages. Acknowledging the differences across regions, the manual also includes a series of recommendations for communication with several segments of the population and on potentially sensitive topics.

Sources: Author's own work, based on https://vnk.fi/en/central-government-communications-guidelines and Costa Rica's responses to the OECD (2020[7]), 2020 Survey for Centres of Government: Understanding Public Communication

---

Formalising and facilitating co-ordination mechanisms

This section analyses the existing vertical and horizontal co-ordination mechanisms in Jordan in the area of public communication. While OECD evidence identifies challenges to formalising inter-ministerial co-ordination and facilitating information sharing, the reactivation of the national network of spokespeople presents an opportunity to break siloes, optimise communication, and promote peer learning.

At its most basic form, co-ordination can take place horizontally (across government entities or different departments of a same organisation), vertically (from a Prime Minister's office to other ministries or other levels of government), and within a given institution. It sets a framework to support the operational effectiveness of the public sector by establishing processes of inter-governmental consultation, co-operation, and joint decision making, as well as promoting regular information sharing (OECD, 2019[8]). Aligning the work of all concerned actors can also ensure coherence of goals, actions, and messages. Moreover, good co-ordination can create a conducive environment for the sharing of best practices and lessons learned among practitioners. While there is no one-size-fits-all approach, OECD countries have adopted various formal and informal mechanisms to co-ordinate public communication activities. Formal mechanisms are usually those of an official nature, observing a hierarchical path and using official tools such as letters, meetings or committees. In contrast, informal means do not follow any prescribed rules or procedures and therefore provide more flexibility.

In Jordan, MoSMA has progressively adopted a greater role in co-ordinating whole of government communication with line ministries, subnational authorities, and within the PMO. Findings from the OECD survey indicate that MoSMA uses a diverse mix of mechanisms to engage with such entities. These range from the use of cross-government teams, internal circulars, joint press conferences, press releases and media handling plans, to the organisation of informal meetings, calls, emails and the use of messaging platforms. At the time of writing, an activity grid to schedule all announcements from the Government was developed but the extent of its application remains unclear.

While substantive progress has been achieved, there is room to strengthen the role of MoSMA as the leading arm unifying and supporting the work of public entities more systematically. In particular, vertical co-ordination between MoSMA and other levels of government could be regularised through the adoption of formal mechanisms, as interviews underlined that current practices ensue only on an ad hoc basis. OECD survey results also suggest that MoSMA could strengthen its role as the central co-ordinating unit for key strategic functions, such as gathering audience insights, campaigns, media announcements, digital communication and crisis responses.

In particular, there is an opportunity to strengthen the link between MosMA and policy development teams to increase the impact of communication. At the time of writing MoSMA began a process to engage with other units at the PMO to operationalise the reforming of media units. As MoSMA takes on a greater leading role, liaising with policy units will be critical to better inform communication initiatives according to the needs of each policy sector and in turn affect the design and delivery of public services.

At the level of ministries, co-ordination could also be improved to reach its desired potential, as it so far remains ad hoc and informal. According to OECD survey results, co-ordination takes place on an occasional basis on issues ranging from the delivery of internal communication to the implementation of campaigns (see Figure 3.3). Findings from an OECD validation workshop corroborated the absence of a regular dialogue between ministries, where co-operation is sometimes restricted to the start and end date of official Memorandums of Understanding or occurring only at the political level between Secretary Generals. Interviews with stakeholders underlined that these challenges have been perpetuated by leadership changes in various ministries, the reliance on personal relationships, uneven capabilities to share information, and differences in organisational structures and practices. Some of these difficulties were also identified within a given institution in the form of low levels of information sharing between media, communication, and public relation teams.

Figure 3.3. Rate of co-ordination on core communication functions in Jordanian Ministries

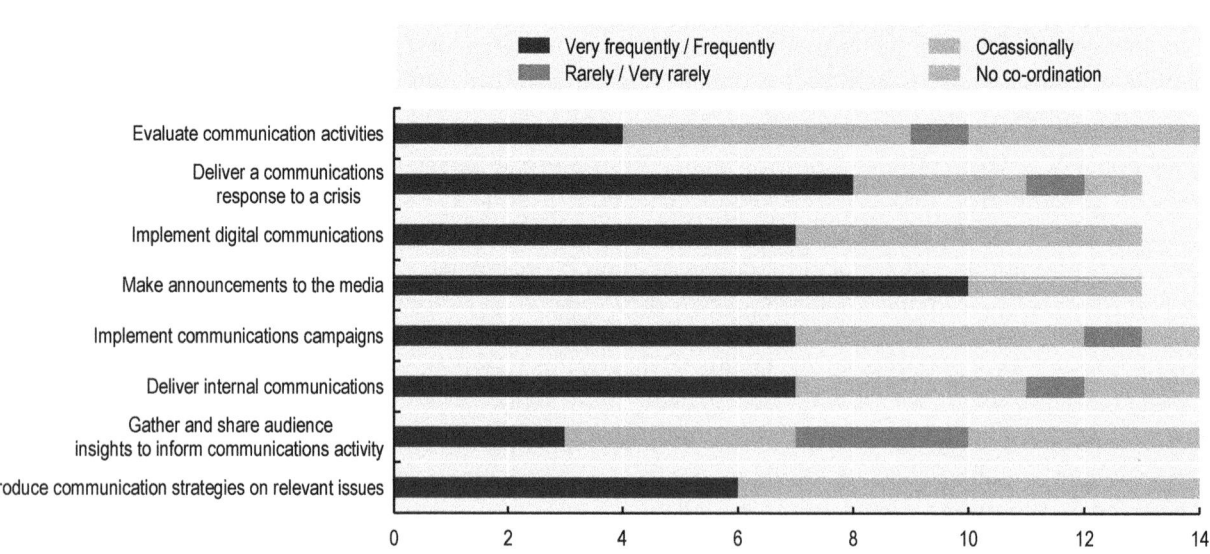

Note: Graph depicts number of ministries, N= 14 ministries. Responses to the question: "How often does the institution co-ordinate with other government ministries, departments and agencies to:"
Source: OECD (2020), Survey for line-ministries in Jordan: Understanding public communication in Jordan.

Broadly, the above-mentioned challenges highlight the need to formalise and facilitate co-ordination at both the strategic and technical level in the country. OECD data suggests that a majority of co-ordination efforts focus on the delivery of internal communication, announcements to the media, crisis responses and strategy development. Thus, co-ordination on technical aspects, such as gathering audience insights, as well as implementing communication campaigns and digital communication could be reinforced. In addition, findings from an OECD validation workshop identified potential for regular co-ordination to not only take place for announcements, but also for campaigns and events. In this regard, the Government of Jordan could consider integrating new digital tools for regular information sharing and the co-deployment of initiatives.

Previously, co-ordination efforts took place as part of the *Network of Spokespersons in the Ministries and Institutions of the Government of Jordan* and through an online platform used to share activities and messages (Alrai, 2018[9]). While these initiatives were temporarily discontinued, at the time of writing MoSMA formalised its re-establishment with the support of the OECD.[5] This is a very positive development as such platforms can support co-operation, peer learning, and best practice exchange, as per OECD good practices (see Box 3.3).

Box 3.3. Examples of bodies supporting public communication co-ordination in OECD and partner countries

The Communications Co-ordination Council of Estonia

To exchange information and organise communication activities, a government communication co-ordination council meets every week in Stenbock House. The council is responsible for co-ordinating whole-of-government communications, organising its working methods, providing consultation to the Government Office in amending and establishing legal acts pertaining to government communication and discussing and adopting positions on key policy issues. The meetings of the council are led by the director of government communication and include heads of communication units from key line-ministries.

The Inter-Ministerial Working Group of Norway

In 2015, an inter-ministerial working group was formed under the Prime Minister's Office, comprised of communication advisors from Norwegian ministries, in order to co-ordinate and stimulate increased usage of social media outlets such as Facebook and Twitter at the ministry level. The working group created standards for how the communication departments in ministries employ social media outlets in order to inform and engage with stakeholders.

The Network of Public Communicators in Morocco

In 2017, and with the support of the OECD, the Ministry of Economy, Finance and Administrative Reform established a network of public communication officers to support the public sector modernisation and open government agenda. It includes representatives from all ministries to exchange on communication approaches as well as related challenges and opportunities in promoting transparency and stakeholder participation.

Source: Author's own work based on Estonian Government (2017[10]), Government Communication Handbook, available online at https://pdfroom.com/books/government-communication-handbook/Pe5xQPR1dnN

The Government of Jordan could consider the formalisation of the network of spokespeople through the creation of a ministerial decree that sets out its vision and through a regular meeting schedule. To ensure the continuity of activities, MoSMA could also contemplate engaging in a consultation exercise with its members to establish a joint mandate with formal objectives, working methods, calendar of meetings and shared digital tools and channels for engagement between peers. Together with capacity building trainings, this platform could help address skill gaps and foster co-ordination on technical policy aspects.

Developing a whole-of-government communication strategy and strengthening the design, implementation and evaluation of ministerial strategies

This section will explore efforts in Jordan towards establishing a unified vision for public communication across government. It will do so by analysing current practices to develop and implement Ministerial strategies, as well as the role of MoSMA in guiding such endeavours. At present, challenges in Jordan remain in terms of establishing a whole-of-government framework, designing quality strategies, ensuring their implementation and translating strategies into actionable plans.

An overarching public communication strategy can help unify efforts under a single vision for the attainment of short, medium and long-term goals. It can also optimise operations and increase the effectiveness of efforts to inform citizens on government action, their rationale and benefits. The use of such documents is particularly important given the specific features of public communication that separate it from other forms of political messaging, where government entities have a responsibility to remain neutral and serve the public interest (Gelders and Ihlen, 2010[2]). In addition, a strategy helps establish more coherent and relevant messaging, the absence of which can be counterproductive, increasing the distance between citizens and public authorities and engendering negative attitudes towards certain policies and services (Kim and Krishna, 2018[11]).

A communication strategy can be defined as a written document adopted for the medium to long term that sets out a strategic framework for all communication activities (OECD, 2020[7]). It outlines the "who", "what" and "why" of activities across the communication cycle, including their planning, co-ordination, implementation and evaluation. Strategies also ensure that various components (audiences, messages, channels, etc.) are directed towards the achievement of clear and predefined short, medium and long-term objectives. Moreover, they provide an overarching approach for the adoption and implementation of action-oriented communication plans and initiatives. For them to be impactful, they need to be accompanied by plans to operationalise the vision with details about the "when" and "how" of activities, by assigning concrete actions, dates, as well as roles and responsibilities (OECD, 2020[7]).

While this list is not exhaustive, some of the key elements for the effective development of strategies and plans include:

- **Setting SMART objectives:** Objectives in nature should be specific, measurable, attainable, realistic, and with a clear timeframe. All content developed should be designed to deliver progress towards the achievement of these goals.
- **Establishing clear roles, responsibilities and accountability lines**: For every aspect of the communication plan, it should be clear who is responsible for its delivery, and who must provide input and approval, as well as the timeline for doing so. Those with overall responsibility "should work closely with colleagues to ensure that these timelines are realistic and that all parties are aware of their responsibilities" (OECD/OGP, 2019[12]).
- **Responding to the needs of different audiences**: It is important to bear in mind how the key messages can best be deployed to reach all audiences. The use of audience insights to inform the development of a strategy is key in this regard, and can support a more tailored choice of channels for engagement.
- **Basing activities on robust evidence:** In order to maximise impact, strategies and plans need to rely on robust research, data and insights that will help assess understandings and perceptions of government actions and reforms. These will help shape tailored messages and targeted programmes, while establishing a baseline for communication.

- **Setting monitoring and evaluation mechanisms:** These mechanisms provide a way to measure the impact of activities and identify areas for improvement. A regular reporting schedule should be built, for example on a quarterly basis, "to assess progress against targets and adjust timelines or mobilise additional resources where needed" (OECD/OGP, 2019[12]). There should also be clear feedback channels in place for participants to raise questions and concerns and inform about potential delays (OECD, 2020[13]).
- **Engagement:** engaging with a variety of stakeholders in the development of strategies and plans is key to ensure they respond to various needs.

In practice, several OECD countries have adopted communication strategies. Indeed, out of 36 centres of government, more than half (65%) say they have a government-wide public communication strategy or policy (OECD, 2017[14]). While they differ in terms of content, they share a number of the above-mentioned elements to guide the implementation of a strategic communication (see Box 3.4 for examples of public communication strategies).

Box 3.4. Examples of public communication strategies and plans in OECD countries

Colombia

The Government of Colombia published a whole-of-government communication strategy in early 2020. It maps the main communication challenges in the country, stressing the importance of making messages relevant and impactful for citizens in the midst of the present information deluge. It also sets out the strategic objectives under the main principle of using this function to provide evidence on the links between government action and citizens' expectations. In doing so, the document calls for communicators to design initiatives from a rational and emotional perspective, to prove that they listen, propose and act. It also includes key messages, establishes a work methodology, proposes monitoring and evaluation indicators and outlines the next steps for ministries to create their own plans.

United Kingdom

The annual Government Communication Plan outlines what communication professionals across Government will collectively deliver to support the UK Government achieve its priority outcomes. The plan was approved in 2019 and focuses on raising communication standards, strengthening democracy and delivering for local communities. The 2019/20 plan highlights high-profile campaigns contributing towards the Government's ambition of "building a country that works for everyone". The work and the standards Government Communication Service (GCS) practitioners adhere to in their work is also outlined.

Source: Based on survey responses from the *OECD Report on Public Communication: The Global Context and the Way Forward*; https://communication-plan.gcs.civilservice.gov.uk/wp-content/uploads/2019/04/Government-Communication-Plan-2019.pdf.

In Jordan, while standard operating procedures in some media units are available, a whole-of-government communication strategy does not yet exist at the CoG. Discussions with stakeholders during the OECD fact-finding mission indicated that ministerial-level policy announcements often focus on the media coverage of one-off statements. They are not typically guided by a long-term vision to achieve broader policy objectives, nor rely on a planned dissemination scheme across multiple channels according to pre-agreed messaging. Developing such a document and ensuring it is linked with adequate human and financial resources for its implementation would help the country move towards a more strategic and proactive approach to communication.

Nonetheless, MoSMA has supported the development of strategic documents to guide the implementation of specific media interventions. The country's first media reform vision (2011-15) aimed to foster an environment supportive of an independent media and to strengthen the existing legal framework governing this sector (UNESCO, 2015[15]). Efforts by MoSMA are currently underway to develop a new strategy in this regard with a view to strengthening relationships with media actors across the country (Almalakatv, 2020[16]).[6] The Government of Jordan has also created several thematic strategies on specific policy issues, including the recently approved Media and Information Literacy National Strategy (2020-23).

With regard to Jordanian ministries, OECD survey results indicate that all 14 ministries report having a strategy, with only 2 institutions having shared a written document (see Box 3.5). Nonetheless, validation interviews noted confusion among ministries between the objectives of communication strategies, plans, and campaigns. Several challenges were also raised in regards to the design and implementation of strategies in this regard. OECD survey results revealed that public authorities face difficulties in designing impactful strategies and ensuring their implementation given the limited availability of human and financial resources. This aligns with findings from a validation workshop underlining that capabilities to design strategies vary significantly, from entities not operationalising these documents to those that engage in extensive media monitoring exercises to support some of its components. An additional challenge was raised in regards to the static nature of these documents, where it is often difficult to adjust the activities, budgets, and timelines therein to unexpected events. Overall, these difficulties together highlight scope to develop more standardised and professional strategies, align practices across ministries, and translate strategies into action plans that can lead to impact through effective implementation, monitoring, and evaluation.

Box 3.5. Example from the Ministry of Tourism in Jordan

The Tourism Media Strategy sets out as its overall mission and vision to improve Jordan's competitive position and shift it to the forefront of global tourism destinations. It outlines an implementation framework for activities focusing on partnerships with journalists, media professionals, bloggers, and activists in the tourism sector to achieve the objectives therein. The strategy also links existing initiatives with the Ministry of Education and Higher Education to promote youth employment in this important sector and ensure appropriate qualification and training of the human force working (local communities, taxi drivers, restaurant and hotel employees, etc.).

In addition, the Department of Tourism outlines several measures to make information readily available to the public. For instance, the Ministry seeks to regularly monitor the reactions and impressions of tourists of their visits to Jordan on tourism websites (Lonely Planet, Airbnb). Its strategy also places an important focus on the Ministry's website, to provide a 24/7 service to all tourists in different languages (in addition to Arabic and English, Russian, French and Spanish).

Source: Author's own work based on the OECD (2020), Survey for line-ministries in Jordan: Understanding public communication in Jordan.

In terms of the objectives highlighted in ministerial strategies, there is also an opportunity to increase the role of communication for transparency and participation. While a majority of OECD survey respondents consider strengthening trust by promoting transparency (71%) as a priority objective therein, less than a third do so for promoting stakeholder participation. In general, strategies primarily focus on raising awareness (79%) and improving the perception of public services (71%) (see Figure 3.4). A positive trend also signals that half of the respondents consider expanding reach to certain types of stakeholders (50%) as an important goal. Therefore, the Government of Jordan could consider focusing communication objectives on opening new spaces for participation, communicating about these opportunities and ensuring the integration of relevant stakeholders, in line with the provisions of the OECD Recommendation of the Council on Open Government (2017[17]).

Figure 3.4. Most important objectives of public communication strategies from line ministries in Jordan

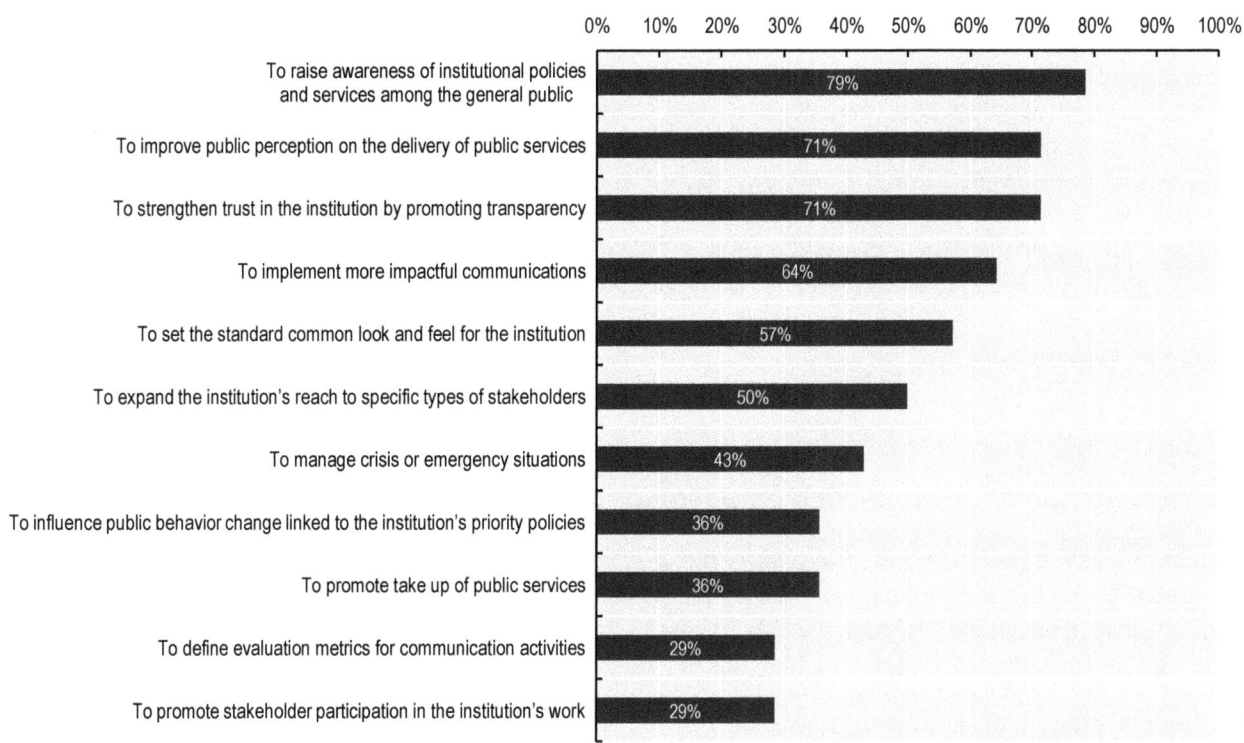

Note: N=14 ministries, response to the question: "If you selected communication strategy, what are its most important objectives?".
Source: OECD (2020), Survey for line-ministries in Jordan: Understanding public communication in Jordan.

In response to these challenges, MoSMA could consider the development of a whole-of-government public communication strategy setting out a mid to long-term shared vision. It would not only help institutionalise procedures and strengthen MoSMA's mandate as the central entity for public communication, but it would also guide the development of ministerial strategies under a common set of goals. This shift, however, will require an investment in developing internal capacities on core competencies, such as planning and messaging, audience insights, digital communication, campaigns, and evaluation. It will also require strengthening co-ordination, translating the strategy into an action plan, as well as guaranteeing the needed financial and human resources to ensure its implementation.

In addition to developing strategies and plans, efforts could also focus on providing support toward their effective implementation. A first mapping could be conducted to make sure that all public entities in Jordan have a written public communication strategy and plan. This could be complemented with capacity building activities to develop skills for the development, implementation, monitoring and evaluation of such documents. In this respect, MoSMA's current advisory role will be an important factor for continued success (see Box 3.6 on examples of role of CoGs in this regard). This process could help generate consistency among all strategies and ensure that their objectives are SMART, linked to broader policy goals and translatable into outcomes. As done by the Government of South Australia, an additional measure could include the creation of a template for ministerial communication strategies (Department of Premier and Cabinet, n.d.[18]).

> **Box 3.6. Ecuador's committee for the approval and review of communication plans**
>
> The General Secretariat of Communications in Ecuador, located under the Prime Minister's Office, is in charge of whole-of-government communication. In its capacity, the Secretariat is also responsible for the review and approval of all ministerial communication plans to ensure that activities are in line with the overarching national strategy. To achieve its mandate, and in support of its advisory role, the Secretariat created an internal Communication Plan Review Committee (or "*Comité de Revisión de Planes de Comunicación*" in Spanish) to review, analyse and approve ministerial directives. In this respect, the committee has reviewed a total of 110 documents, from which 65 Communication Plans have been approved and 17 requests for communication investment projects endorsed.
>
> Source: Author's own work, based on Ecuador's responses to the OECD (2020[7]), OECD Centre of Government Survey: Understanding Public Communication.

Addressing human resource and competency gaps

Adequate levels of skilled human resources are a *sine qua non* condition for a strategic communication approach. While the restructuring of this function has gradually established dedicated structures at the level of ministries, there is considerable diversity in terms of capacities and skills. OECD survey respondents furthermore underlined that human resource management remains the most challenging competency to establish a two-way dialogue with citizens. This section will therefore explore potential avenues to strengthen human resource management through an initial assessment of existing hiring, training, and professional development practices.

Strategic human resource management can help governments improve the efficiency, quality, and responsiveness of public services by aligning capabilities toward the attainment of organisational goals (OECD, n.d.[19]). This is no different in the field of public communication, where its evolution due to the introduction of novel technologies and practices calls for an increasingly skilled worked force. From the hiring stage to that of performance evaluation, there is a critical role in "developing communication skillsets of staff and in recognising [...] the increasingly specialised nature of communication knowledge and expertise" (Sanders and Canel, 2013[1]). This is all the more important considering the growing concern among OECD countries that "the skill sets commonly used within the public sector may no longer be keeping up with the fast pace of change in the societies they aim to support and improve" (OECD, n.d.[19]).

The OECD Recommendation of the Council on Public Service Leadership and Capability emphasises the importance of building adequate levels of skills to ensure the transformation of a political vision into policy action (OECD, 2019[8]). The Recommendation summarises 14 principles to foster a value-driven, trusted, capable, responsive and adaptive public service, suggesting governments invest in core capabilities by (OECD, 2019[8]):

- Continuously identifying skills and competencies needed to transform political vision into services that deliver value to society.
- Attracting and retaining employees with the skills and competencies required.
- Recruiting, selecting, and promoting candidates through transparent, open and merit-based processes.
- Developing the necessary skills and competencies by creating a learning culture and environment in the public service.
- Assessing, rewarding and recognising performance, talent and initiative.

In Jordan, public entities benefit from a relatively established body of communicators, both politically appointed and members of the civil service. As detailed above, Jordan has undertaken, and continues to conduct, multiple initiatives aimed at restructuring its communication model. Further investments in the capacity of communication units and the professionalisation of communicators are necessary for its transition to a more strategic communication approach. Indeed, this is all the more important as the lack of or insufficient human resources was selected as the most important challenge to carrying out core communication competencies by over half of responding ministries on average (53%).

While all surveyed ministries report having dedicated full-time staff, the development of job posts and recruiting practices could be further consolidated. In terms of skills, findings reveal uneven practices regarding the hiring in media units, as only 8 out of 14 ministries have identified a framework or list of core competencies. These findings align with those from an OECD validation workshop stressing that the lack of written and robust job descriptions is at present exacerbating issues in terms of performance evaluations. At the time of writing, MoSMA noted the creation of a manual with recruiting guidelines, but signalled that this has yet to be implemented across public entities in Jordan.

Despite the growing consolidation of media units, several challenges have also obstructed progress in terms of strategic human resource management. First, the lack of operational structures has presented challenges in terms of defining the role of communication teams. Second, slow recruitment processes have impeded the acquisition of talent to fulfil technical roles. Third, turnover levels resulting from past reshuffles has impacted institutional memory, the build-up of expertise, and consistency of a given Ministry's approach. To address such challenges, developing standards for the communication profession and defining a core capability framework for the job posts could solidify gains achieved thus far in terms of establishing media units. At the time of writing, the Civil Service Bureau initiated efforts to develop such a framework in acknowledgement of public communication as a priority lever of government.

Given the uneven resources available across ministries, the Government could also benefit from developing a comprehensive training programme focused on key strategic functions. While 86% of survey respondents reported that communication teams receive training, they also noted the need for technical assistance to better respond to the needs of the citizens (see Figure 3.5). These findings align with OECD survey responses underscoring variances in terms of the background and skills of these teams regarding their degree of specialisation in the fields of journalism, marketing, design, and public relations. Interviews with stakeholders revealed that capacity-building activities in Jordan are mostly conducted on an ad-hoc basis with a limited focus on campaigns and digital communication, in addition to being dispersed and without a concrete programme supporting their institutionalisation. At present, these opportunities are centralised and provided by the PMO, which also deals with requesting specialised technical assistance from external actors and donors.

Figure 3.5. Share of ministries in Jordan that receive communication specific training

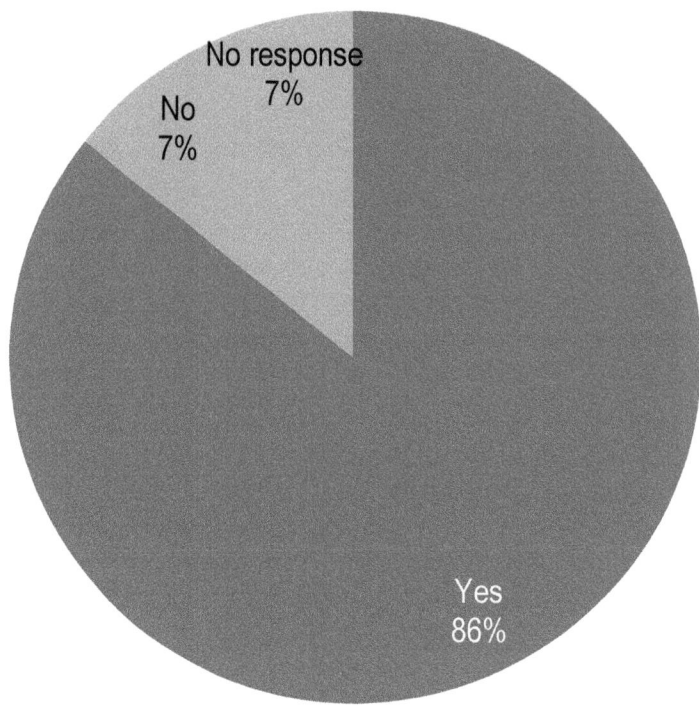

Note: N= 14 Ministries, responses to the question: "do the members of the communications team or relevant officer have communications training?".
Source: OECD (2020), Survey for line-ministries in Jordan: Understanding public communication in Jordan.

In terms of skill development, MoSMA could address existing challenges by identifying capacity gaps and recommending a training curricula built around core communication functions. To this end, an initial mapping of skill gaps could allow MoSMA to request relevant trainings according to the needs of different institutions. Such workshops could focus on modernising core skills, such as audience insights, online engagement and interactivity, and new evaluation methodologies. In time, the Government of Jordan could consider formalising training into institutionalised programmes or academies for public communicators as done in several OECD countries (see Box 3.7). Ultimately, future efforts could focus on promoting the reach, relevance, and sustainability of training and professional development opportunities.

> **Box 3.7. Public Communication skill academies in OECD countries**
>
> **The UK Government Communication Service Academy**
>
> Through its vision to build professional standards across government, the *Government Communication Service Academy* in the United Kingdom aims to improve the performance of communicators and help build their careers through a robust offer of trainings and online resources.
>
> The Professional Standards Team works with the heads of each communication discipline to design and deliver relevant development and training opportunities. Through its online and day courses, the academy provides workshops on themes such as campaign excellence; understanding disinformation; crisis communication; behavioural insights; and presenting with impact. It makes its offer readily available to communicators through an online site centralising all upcoming workshops. The academy also collaborates with external professional bodies, such as the Public Relations Consultants Association (PRCA) and the Market Research Society (MRS), to expand its offer of webinars and learning resources.
>
> The UK's Government Communication Service also carries out an annual skills survey to measure the capabilities of its teams and uses the results to tailor professional development sessions to improve skills and resources across the entire function. These efforts operate under a formal career framework for its staff to manage their professional development and continue to build their competency and expertise, while gaining relevant experience.
>
> **The Academy for Government Communication in the Netherlands**
>
> The Academy for Government Communications assists the central government in supporting the professionalisation and training of civil servants in the communication function. It is the knowledge and expertise centre in the field of government communication and is part of the Public and Communication Service of the Ministry of General Affairs. It helps communication staff maintain their professional knowledge, keeping them updated on respective trends within their fields, developing learning pathways as well as creating inter-ministerial networks.
>
> All training courses are bundled in a coherent training programme, called the "Learning Line". The goal is to create a more uniform training of communication staff, government-wide employability and networking. The courses are only available to civil servants. The Academy offers a wide range of courses and trainings that include an introduction course on Communication at the National Government; professional trainings for Experienced Editors, Press Officers, and Speech Writers; modules on Behavior, Visual Communication and Professional Environmental Management; learning routes on Strategic Advice and Connecting Leadership; a masterclass on Theme Inspiration; as well as courses on Podcasts and Content Creation. The Academy also provides training for Policy Officers, in collaboration with the PBLQ ROI training centre in The Hague.
>
> Moreover, the Academy organises meetings to stimulate knowledge sharing through webinars on current subject themes, annual conferences for government communication, as well as learning networks around specific themes (such as inclusion or Instagram) in which colleagues share knowledge through online meetings and record them for further dissemination. In addition to training courses, learning networks and knowledge webinars, the Academy offers an online platform, "Ons CommunicatieRijk", in which communication professionals can share knowledge, ask questions and find colleagues. The Academy can also be found on Twitter, LinkedIn, and a monthly newsletter is published.
>
> A special service carried out by the Academy worth noting is the management of the Communication Pool, a group of 40 strategic communication advisers and press secretaries, mainly self-employed, who

have signed a framework agreement with the central government. These advisers can be hired by ministries whenever they are short on staff, or for specific strategic jobs or projects.

Source: Author's own work based on https://gcs.civilservice.gov.uk/academy/; https://www.communicatierijk.nl/vakkennis/aanbod-academie-voor-overheidscommunicatie; https://www.government.nl/ministries/ministry-of-general-affairs/organisation

Recognising highly impactful communication practices and initiatives could also help build core capabilities across all public institutions in Jordan. For instance, the Government of Canada recognises communication excellence in the federal public service and celebrates innovative practices through its yearly Communication Awards (see Box 3.8). Publicising the impact of initiatives would not only serve to recognise best practices, reward and incentivise outstanding performance, but it could also help gain approval for more ambitious activities and investments from senior officials.

Box 3.8. Canada's Communications Awards of Excellence

The Communications Awards of Excellence from the Government of Canada recognise outstanding practices and celebrate the achievements of the public communication community. The ceremony, which takes place once a year, is an opportunity for the sharing of lessons learnt, good practices and innovations in the field. The Government recognises excellence under five excellence in communications awards (Team Awards) and five Spotlight Awards (Individual Awards). Following the robust evaluation criteria online, all entities are able to submit their nomination, which are ultimately reviewed by the Communication Community Office and its Steering Committee.

The Communications Awards of Excellence were established in 2019, and have since then served as a platform to set professional standards for communication across Canada.

Source: Author's own work, based on https://www.canada.ca/en/privy-council/services/communications-community-office/communications-awards-excellence.html

Ensuring dedicated financial resources

As the ongoing restructuring aims to transform the work of public communicators in Jordan it will be critical to ensure adequate levels of financial resources. This short section will take stock of the current related challenges in Jordan and make the case for the importance of establishing a dedicated budget in this regard.

Dedicated fund streams are fundamental in translating strategies and initiatives into concrete results. A budget for public communication not only helps ensure the sustainability of efforts, but also attributes tangible value to this function and helps recognise its importance. A strategic communication approach thus relies on setting dedicated budgetary allocations against concrete objectives, linked to government priorities and evaluated against performance indicators. In this regard, the OECD Recommendation on Budget Governance underpins the importance of budgetary efficiency and sets out ten basic principles for their effective design, implementation and evaluation (see Box 3.9).

> **Box 3.9. OECD principles for sound budgetary governance**
>
> 1. Manage budgets within clear, credible and predictable limits for fiscal policy.
> 2. Closely align budgets with the medium-term strategic priorities of government.
> 3. Design the capital budgeting framework in order to meet national development needs in a cost-effective and coherent manner.
> 4. Ensure that budget documents and data are open, transparent and accessible.
> 5. Provide for an inclusive, participative and realistic debate on budgetary choices.
> 6. Present a comprehensive, accurate and reliable account of the public finances.
> 7. Actively plan, manage and monitor budget execution.
> 8. Ensure that performance, evaluation & value for money are integral to the budget process.
> 9. Identify, assess and manage prudently longer-term sustainability and other fiscal risks.
> 10. Promote the integrity and quality of budgetary forecasts, fiscal plans and budgetary implementation through rigorous quality assurance including independent audit.
>
> Source: OECD (2015[20]), Recommendation of the Council on Budgetary Governance, https://www.oecd.org/gov/budgeting/Recommendation-of-the-Council-on-Budgetary-Governance.pdf

As in many OECD countries, Jordan will need to address low levels of available funding for communication activities. Indeed, OECD survey results revealed that the lack of or insufficient funding streams was selected as the second biggest challenge on average to carrying out key functions (46%). With the exception of MoSMA, 5 out of 14 ministries indicate the lack of a dedicated budget for communication as a key issue (see Figure 3.6). Moreover, MoSMA's survey responses revealed a reliance on donor funds to carry out initiatives such as insight gathering, trainings, and campaign design and delivery. Interviews with stakeholders also stressed that the existing procurement framework presents challenges to the contracting of external services due to bureaucratic and unclear procedures.

Figure 3.6. Number of Ministries in Jordan with a dedicated budget for public communication

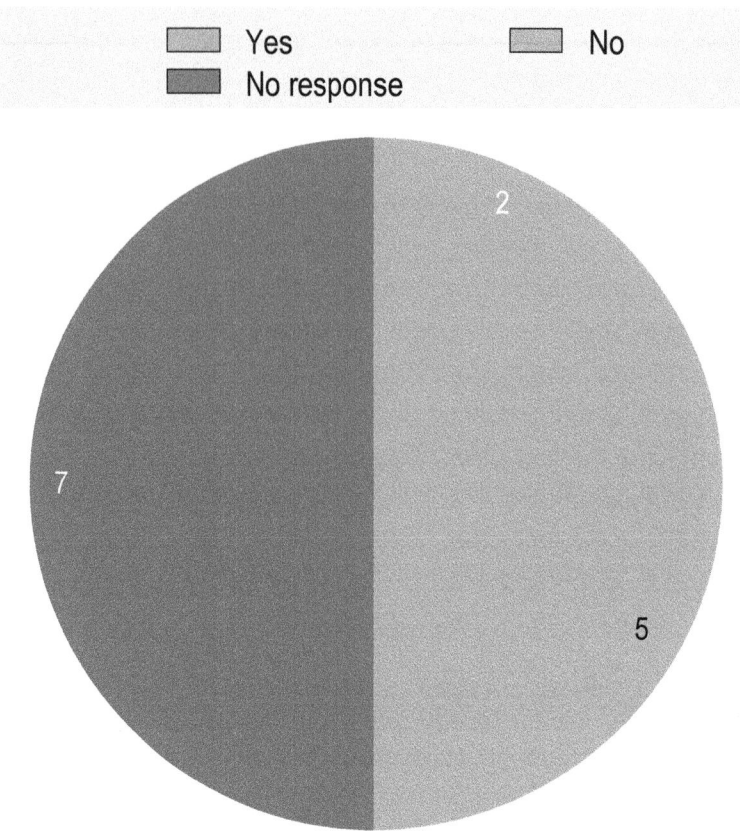

Source: OECD (2020), Survey for line-ministries in Jordan: Understanding public communication in Jordan.

To strengthen the strategic perspective of public communication in Jordan, the Government could consider establishing dedicated budget lines in media units to support the deployment of core communication functions and activities. This will be all the more important to ensure the successful re-structuring of these entities, in particular to enable them to deliver on their new responsibilities. Indeed, dedicated funding streams could help ensure the sustainability of communication initiatives, equip ministries with modernised tools and skills, and change the perception around the value of this function at the highest political levels.

An initial step to address funding gaps could involve a mapping of existing and future financing needs to make the case for investment in public communication tools, capacities and initiatives. To support the business case for communication, efforts could focus on the monitoring and impact evaluation of initiatives currently underway.

Recommendations

The following recommendations provide a roadmap to support the ongoing restructuring of public communication in Jordan. They summarise the main takeaways from the chapter and include potential avenues to move toward a more strategic communication approach.

Strengthening public communication structures in Jordan

- Continue existing efforts to standardise and fully operationalise media units as part of the restructuring of the public communication function in Jordan, allowing for more clarity concerning their roles and responsibilities.
- Formalise communication procedures across ministries through guidelines or decrees, to ensure consistency in the role and mandate of public communicators over time and regardless of changes in leadership. A first step could include scaling efforts to disseminate MoSMA's manual on the organisation of media units, clarifying roles, and responsibilities and codifying processes.

Formalising and facilitating co-ordination mechanisms

- Ensure the continuity of the network of communicators under the co-ordination of MoSMA to facilitate information sharing, align messages and plan join events. MoSMA could consider formalising the network through a decree and engage in a consultation exercise with members to identify and establish a joint mandate with formal objectives, working methods, calendar of activities and digital tools and channels for engagement between peers.
- Expand inter-ministerial dialogue on technical aspects, such as gathering audience insights and digital communications, through the integration of new tools for information sharing and the regularisation of meetings in the framework of the network to foster the exchange of good practices.
- Consider the creation of a centralised information repository where guidelines, manuals and other relevant information can be accessible to all public entities. This will not only support the dissemination of good practices to professionalise the work of units but to institutionalise practices across entities.

Developing a whole-of-government communication strategy and strengthening the design, implementation and evaluation of ministerial strategies

- Develop a whole-of-government public communication strategy, together with an action plan, setting the Government's vision for reform, outlining the main objectives for its achievement and identifying evaluation indicators to measure its success. An overarching strategy and plan could also help guide the development of those at the ministry level, based on a common vision and approach, and provide an implementation roadmap.
- Provide support for the design, implementation and evaluation of ministry-specific communication strategies. This could include the development of guidelines, the deployment of trainings and the establishment of a review committee by MoSMA to approve and evaluate sectoral strategies.
- MoSMA could also consider the development of a template to ensure the translation of ministerial strategies into plans.

Addressing human resource and competency gaps

- Develop and operationalise a dedicated competency framework for the public communication profession in Government to provide clear entry points, requirements for advancement, and opportunities for vertical and horizontal career progression.

- Increase the professional competencies of public communicators through dedicated training programmes on topics such as audience insights, planning, messaging, digital communication, campaigns, and evaluation. An initial mapping of skill gaps could allow MoSMA to design a robust programme for the PMO, which in time could be formalised into a public skills academy or integrated into existing curricula for officials.
- Widely disseminate the newly created recruitment guidelines for the establishment of capabilities within media units and the promotion of professional standards.
- Recognise, award and disseminate highly-impactful communication campaigns and activities across public entities in Jordan.

Ensuring dedicated financial resources

- Establish a dedicated budget for MosMA and media units to support the deployment of core communication functions and activities. Budget allocations could be based on a mapping of funding gaps and an analysis of yearly needs based on communication plans to be developed. To ensure the efficient management of resources, a regular evaluation of funds spent could be envisaged with a focus on increasing the transparency and visibility of results.

References

Almalakatv (2020), *Almalakatv website*, https://www.almamlakatv.com/news/32271-. [6]

Almalakatv (2020), *Minister of Information: An electronic application that provides the most important information and details*, https://www.almamlakatv.com/news/32271-. [16]

Alrai (2018), "غنيمات: توجه لمأسسة عمل دوائر الناطقين الإعلاميين ولا نخشى النقد في حال التقصير - صور - صحيفة الرأي", *Alrai*, http://alrai.com/article/10463604 (accessed on 27 September 2019). [9]

Department of Premier and Cabinet (n.d.), *Government communications*, https://www.dpc.sa.gov.au/responsibilities/government-communications. [18]

Estonian Government (2017), *Government Communication Handbook*, https://www.valitsus.ee/sites/default/files/content-editors/failid/government_communication_handbook_eng_13.09.2017.pdf. [10]

Gelders, D. and Ø. Ihlen (2010), "Government communication about potential policies: Public relations, propaganda or both?", *Public Relations Review*, Vol. 36/1, pp. 59-62, http://dx.doi.org/10.1016/j.pubrev.2009.08.012. [2]

IFAC and CIPFA (2014), *International Framework: Good Governance in the Public Sector*, https://www.ifac.org/knowledge-gateway/contributing-global-economy/publications/international-framework-good-governance-public-sector. [5]

Kim, S. and A. Krishna (2018), "Unpacking Public Sentiment Toward the Government: How Citizens' Perceptions of Government Communication Strategies Impact Public Engagement, Cynicism, and Communication Behaviors in South Korea", *International Journal of Strategic Communication*, Vol. 12/3, pp. 215-236, http://dx.doi.org/10.1080/1553118x.2018.1448400. [11]

Luoma-aho, V. and M. Canel (eds.) (2020), *The Handbook of Public Sector Communication*, Wiley, http://dx.doi.org/10.1002/9781119263203. [3]

OECD (2021), *OECD Report on Public Communication: The Global Context and the Way Forward*, OECD Publishing, Paris, https://doi.org/10.1787/22f8031c-en. [4]

OECD (2020), *OECD Centre of Government Survey 2020: Understanding Public Communication*. [7]

OECD (2020), *Supporting Open Government at the Local Level in Jordan*, OECD, Paris, https://www.oecd.org/gov/open-government/supporting-open-government-at-the-local-level-in-jordan.pdf. [13]

OECD (2019), "Recommendation of the Council on Public Service Leadership and Capability", *OECD Legal Instruments*, OECD-LEGAL-0438, OECD, Paris, https://legalinstruments.oecd.org/en/instruments/OECD-LEGAL-0445. [8]

OECD (2017), *Organisation and functions at the centre of government: Centre Stage II*. [14]

OECD (2017), "Recommendation of the Council on Open Government", *OECD Legal Instruments*, OECD-LEGAL-0438, OECD, Paris, https://legalinstruments.oecd.org/en/instruments/OECD-LEGAL-0438. [17]

OECD (2015), "Recommendation of the Council on Budgetary Governance", *OECD Legal Instruments*, OECD/LEGAL/0410, OECD, Paris, https://www.oecd.org/gov/budgeting/Recommendation-of-the-Council-on-Budgetary-Governance.pdf. [20]

OECD (n.d.), *Skills and capacity*, OECD, Paris, https://www.oecd.org/gov/pem/skills-and-capacity.htm (accessed on 13 September 2021). [19]

OECD/OGP (2019), *Communicating Open Government: A How-To Guide*, Open Government Partnership, https://www.opengovpartnership.org/documents/communicating-open-government-a-how-to-guide-oecd-ogp/. [12]

Sanders, K. and M. Canel (2013), *Government Communication: Cases and challenges*, Bloomsbury Academic. [1]

UNESCO (2015), "Assessment of media development in Jordan", https://en.unesco.org/partnerships/foe/support-media-jordan (accessed on 23 September 2019). [15]

Notes

[1] Public communication commitments in the *Jordan 2025 Vision*, the *National Renaissance Plan* (2019-2020), the *Indicative Executive Program* (2021-2023), and the forthcoming *Government Economic Recovery Priorities Plan*, among others.

[2] Centre of government is defined as the support structure serving the highest level of the executive branch of government (presidents, prime ministers and their equivalents).

[3] Some of these responsibilities are shared with other public institutions, including the National Center for Security and Crisis Management, Media departments across the government, the Ministry of Tourism, and the Ministry of Foreign Affairs. Shared responsibilities mainly focus on the formulation and implementation of sector specific campaigns and crisis responses.

[4] Staff within MoSMA work full time on campaigns, digital communication, crisis communication, countering disinformation and media engagement, whilst specific individuals handle the strategy, internal communication and insight gathering elements of work. Evaluation, stakeholder participation, and trainings are conducted on an ad-hoc basis.

[5] In the framework of the Citizens' Voice Project, the OECD supported MoSMA in the establishment of a network of spokespeople in the country. This network is meant to serve as a platform to promote formal partnerships between institutions, scale the sharing of good practices and provide training to even capacity levels across institutions.

[6] The OECD understands that the Ministry of State for Media Affairs (MOSMA) is planning to develop a new national strategy for media. The strategy may ultimately include areas focused on legal reforms, the media watchdog, the JPA, a media complaints commission, disinformation and community media, etc.

4 Developing more strategic use of key communication competencies in Jordan

Following an assessment of internal communication mechanisms in Jordan, this chapter will explore current practices and gaps in key communication competencies, including the use of audience insights, digital communication and evaluation. It will also provide recommendations on how such capabilities can contribute to increased transparency, integrity, accountability and stakeholder participation.

Introduction

The field of public communication is in constant evolution. Technological shifts and their impact on media ecosystems are constantly transforming the way governments reach and interact with citizens. At the same time, the COVID-19 crisis is accelerating these transformations at an unprecedented speed and scale. Its profound implications have demonstrated just how critical equipping public institutions with the right communication capabilities can be to ensure the continuity of operations, share lifesaving information and mobilise a wide diversity of stakeholders.

As part of the analytical framework, the OECD recognises the effective deployment of core communication competencies as a precondition to foster a two-way dialogue with citizens. These include audience insights, digital communication as well as evaluation. When deployed strategically, they can aid public institutions in generating buy-in around key reforms strengthening transparency, as well as opening up opportunities for stakeholders to participate in the policy cycle.

Recognising these benefits, initial efforts in Jordan are underway to strengthen such competencies across the public administration in the framework of the ongoing restructuring process. While progress has been achieved to date, Figure 4.1 illustrates how a majority of ministries continue to face challenges in terms of effectively deploying campaigns, producing strategies, and reaching audiences through digital channels. OECD survey results also reveal that most respondents attribute these challenges to a lack of or insufficiency of skilled staff (53% on average), financial resources (46%), and co-ordination issues (23%).

Figure 4.1. Share of ministries in Jordan selecting the below challenges to implementing core communication competencies

Most challenging communication competencies selected by line ministries in Jordan

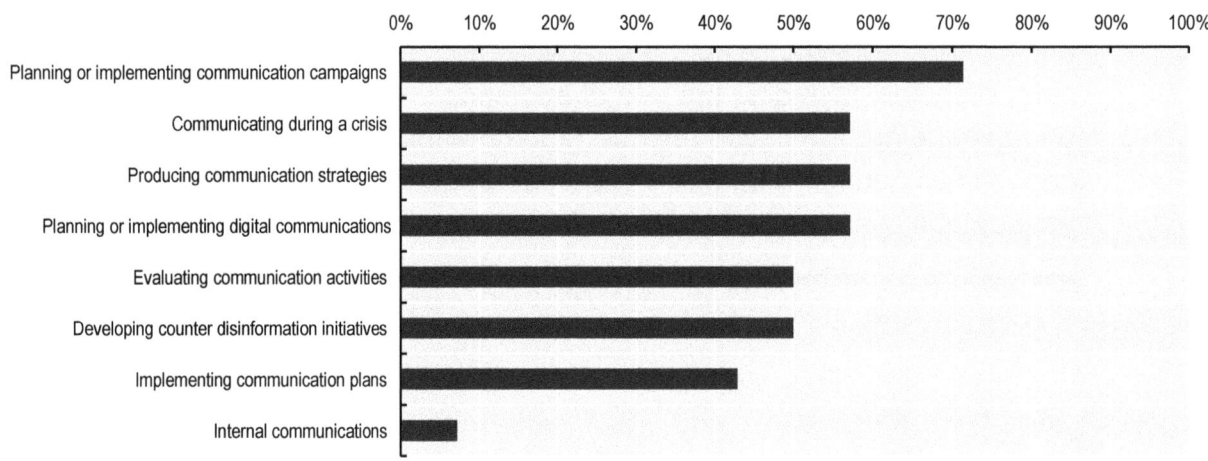

Source: OECD (2020), Survey for ministries in Jordan: Understanding public communication in Jordan.

Against this backdrop, the following section will analyse these challenges in greater depth and explore avenues for the Government to strengthen these key competencies.

Utilising audience insights to maximise reach and impact

Insight gathering is understood as the conducting of research into different segments of the population to gain a deeper understanding of their motivations, impeding factors, fears, media consumption habits, and levels of understanding on a particular subject (OECD, 2020[1]). Notably, it can aid in the delivery of personalised messaging to raise awareness of key reforms and change behaviours.

As in several OECD countries, the Government of Jordan is at the early stages of establishing the practice of gathering and using audience insights systematically. While this function is not currently institutionalised, MoSMA notes that it regularly interacts with behavioural insight experts from academia, civil society, and international organisations for the design of communication material. At the level of ministries, these practices are slowly emerging, with a focus on the use of limited external data, and where they exist, OECD survey data reveals they are conducted on an occasional (7 out of 14) or a rare to very rare basis (2 out of 14). Furthermore, and as Figure 4.2 illustrates, only 36% of public institutions in Jordan draw on such data to identify key messages and preferred means of communication. OECD survey data also underlines room to tailor communications to the needs, expectations and habits of traditionally underrepresented groups,[1] as close to one-fourth of ministries do not yet do so.

Figure 4.2. Criteria used by Jordanian public institutions for the selection of public communication channels

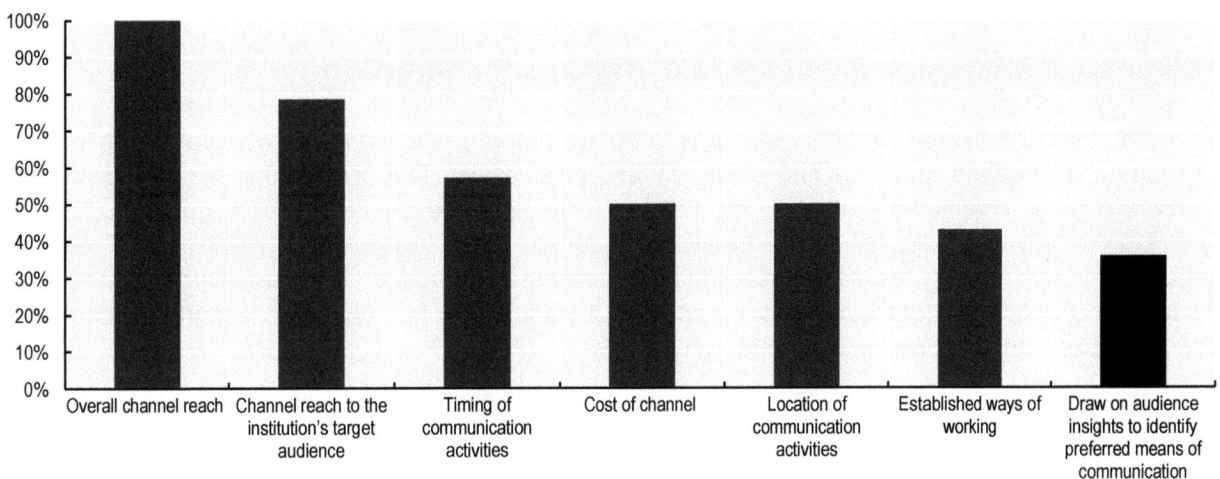

Source: OECD (2020), Survey for ministries in Jordan: Understanding public communication in Jordan.

A first step to professionalising the competency of audience insights across government will require dedicating financial resources and building internal capabilities for its consistent application through trainings and guidelines. These efforts could be complemented with the creation of a central hub within the PMO to monitor and collect behavioural data across different policy areas to in turn inform the selection of channels, messages and objectives of communication (see Box 4.1 for an example).

> **Box 4.1. Examples of central insight gathering in OECD countries during the covid-19 crisis**
>
> **United Kingdom**
>
> The UK Government communication service is promoting the deployment of data and insight-driven messages through daily insights and evaluation dashboard for public communicators. This platform is informed by daily polling and pulse surveys collecting information on public mood, social conversation around the topic, and the state of public opinion on government measures. UK GCS also conducts 3 to 4 weekly focus groups to gather qualitative insights and in turn, directly share this information across government as well as inform the direction of their COVID-19 communication strategy and campaigns.
>
> **The Netherlands**
>
> The Government conducts regular sentiment analysis to advise on the development of health-related measures and COVID-19 communication campaigns. For instance, a central unit has been collecting information since the beginning of the pandemic on the levels of trust in government information. The Government has also focused on analysing how specific words and terms resonate with the general public to simplify language in their messaging.
>
> Source: Author's own work, based on OECD (2020[2])

Leveraging the interactivity benefits of digital communication

The digital transformation of the public sector is "propelling more participatory, innovative and agile forms of governance targeting goals beyond efficiency and productivity" (OECD, 2020[1]). At the same time, citizens are more connected than ever before and have higher expectations from governments with regards to the delivery of services. Unlike traditional channels, digital technologies (which go beyond social media alone) are providing meaningful ways to communicate and engage with stakeholders in the design and delivery of policies. These benefits are prompting a gradual shift from unilateral sharing of information to a more citizen-driven communication (Murphy, 2019[3]).

In Jordan, digital channels have become one of the primary means for the Government to communicate with the public. This trend has become more prominent in recent months as activities have migrated to the online sphere following the COVID-19 pandemic. At the central level, MoSMA makes use of an official government website (http://www.pm.gov.jo/), dedicated campaign microsites (https://your.gov.jo/ & https://corona.moh.gov.jo/ar), in addition to social media platforms and online advertisements to communicate. A similar trend can be observed at the level of ministries, where most institutions have begun consolidating an online presence through various channels (see Table 4.1).

Table 4.1. Mapping the online presence of Jordanian Public Institutions

Institution	Facebook	Twitter	Institutional website
Prime Minister's Office	https://www.facebook.com/PMOJO/	@PrimeMinistry	http://www.pm.gov.jo/
Minister of State for Media Affairs	https://www.facebook.com/amjad.o.adaileh	@Amjad_O_Adaileh	http://www.pm.gov.jo/
Ministry of Culture	https://www.facebook.com/culture.gov.jo/	@cultureminstry	https://culture.gov.jo/
Ministry of Transport	https://www.facebook.com/MinistryOfTransportJo	@Mtransport_jo	http://www.mot.gov.jo/
Ministry of Labor	https://www.facebook.com/MOL.gov.jo	@MofLabour	http://www.mol.gov.jo/
Ministry of Justice	https://www.facebook.com/mojgovjo	@MOJ_Jor	http://www.moj.gov.jo/
Ministry of Awqaf and	https://www.facebook.com/AwqafJordan	@AwqafJordan	http://www.awqaf.gov.jo/

Religious Affairs			
Ministry of Tourism	https://www.facebook.com/mota.jordan	@MOTA_Jordan	http://www.tourism.jo/
Ministry of Entrepreneurship and Digital Economy	https://www.facebook.com/MoDEEJO/	@MoDEEJO	https://www.modee.gov.jo/
Ministry of Higher Education	https://www.facebook.com/mohejordan	@mohegovjo	http://www.mohe.gov.jo/
Ministry of Education	https://www.facebook.com/edugovjo	@edugovjo	https://moe.gov.jo/
Ministry of Trade and Industry	https://www.facebook.com/mit.gov.jo/	@MIT_HKJ	https://www.mit.gov.jo/
Ministry of Planning and International Cooperation	https://www.facebook.com/MoPIC.JORDAN/	@MoPIC_Jordan	https://www.mop.gov.jo/
Ministry of Health	https://www.facebook.com/mohgovjordan	@mohgovjo	https://moh.gov.jo/
Jordan Investment Commission	https://www.facebook.com/jordanInvestmentCommission/	@JIC_Investment	https://www.jic.gov.jo/
Social Security Corporation	https://www.facebook.com/JordanSSC	@SSC_Jordan	https://www.ssc.gov.jo/

Source: Author's own work.

While public entities in Jordan continue to work on establishing an online presence, challenges remain in terms of unequal levels of skills and lack of dedicated staff for the management of both institutional websites and social media pages. Interviews with stakeholders revealed that few ministries have dedicated units, whilst other entities conduct ad hoc digital communications managed primarily by the IT manager. Digital skills on interactive social media use, optimising web presence, media monitoring, and online plain language, therefore, tend to vary significantly across ministries. It was also noted that attempts to address talent gaps through the outsourcing of digital services also remains a challenge given the lack of a procurement framework to hire these services.

To this end, building internal capabilities will be critical to leverage the benefits of online platforms to communicate in more immediate and interactive ways with citizens. In addition to specialised trainings, OECD countries such as Canada are establishing communities of practitioners to align practices, encourage the adoption of innovative digital tools, and exchange knowledge (see Box 4.2).

Box 4.2. Digital communication communities of practice in Canada

The Canadian Communications Community Office provides support to public communicators across the country with regards to skill development. As part of its work, it created several thematic communities of practice, led by federal communicators, for its members to share information and tools, discuss common challenges, develop and share new approaches. Recognising the need to catalyse digital technologies for communication, the CCO houses communities in areas such as digital analytics, social media and web community. Communities across different thematic areas of communication gather once a year through the "CCO learning days" to reflect on the opportunities and challenges to professionalise this function.

Source: Communications Community Office of Canada (2019[4]), Annual Report (2019-2020), https://www.canada.ca/en/privy-council/services/communications-community-office/reports/annual-2019-2020.html#toc5.

In terms of the usage of websites, an in-depth analysis of those managed by all survey respondents identified potential avenues to improve their contribution to participation and transparency. While they are generally aligned and user-friendly, access to relevant information could be simplified, as it is often scattered. Building on the existing practice to publish progress reports with relevant statistics on projects, investments and policies, this information together with a calendar of events and other relevant documents, could be consolidated in a single section and updated regularly to promote accessibility. For websites to reap their full interactivity benefits, ministries could also dedicate a section on public consultations and use these platforms to crowdsource feedback on key policies.

With the growing adoption of social media as a tool for communication, the Government of Jordan could also benefit from using these platforms in a more strategic way. This is all the more important given the large internet (67%) and social media (56%) penetration rate in the country and even more so in the wake of the COVID-19 pandemic (Kemp, 2020[5]). As Figure 4.3 illustrates, the wide adoption of such platforms by public institutions in Jordan underlines the potential to go beyond solely sharing information to open spaces for citizens to engage on issues that matter most to them. Conversely, communication perceived as unresponsive may have the adverse effect of disengaging the public (OECD, 2020[6]).

Figure 4.3. Social media use by Ministries in Jordan

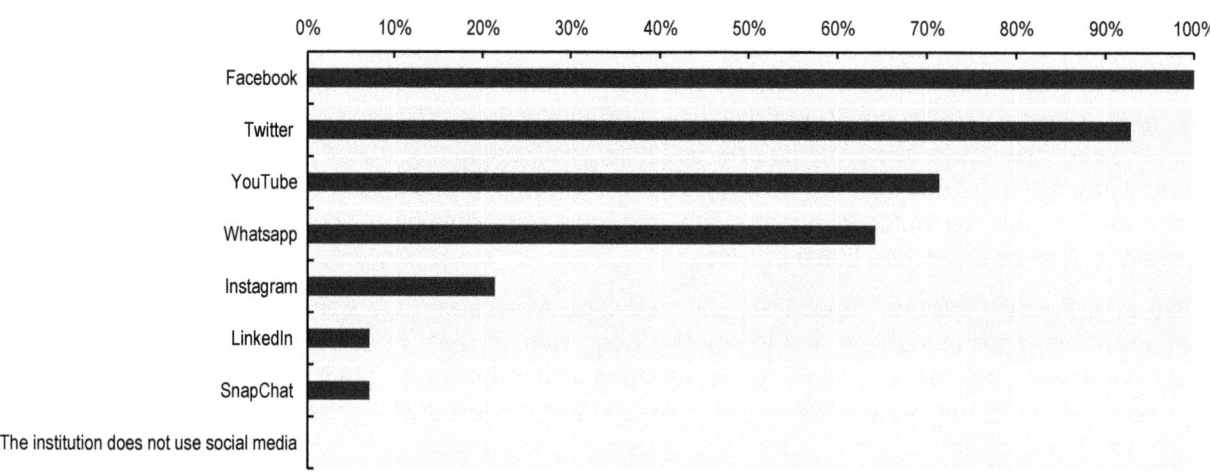

Source: OECD (2020), Survey for ministries in Jordan: Understanding public communication in Jordan.

OECD research indicates that despite the regular use of social media by the government, low levels of engagement remain due to often generic posts and insufficient engagement with public comments. As Table 4.2 illustrates, few institutions actively reply to or interact with citizens. Interestingly, high levels of reach (number of tweets retweeted) coincide with those from institutions with high reply rates or frequent publishing levels, suggesting that the transparent disclosure of information and a two-way communication can help reinforce trust and incentivise citizens to progressively engage. To this end, the Government of Jordan could follow similar recommendations from those above aimed at websites to enhance the participation aspect of these platforms.

Table 4.2. Government use of Facebook and Twitter in Jordan (2020)

	Facebook followers as share of population (%)	Twitter followers as share of population (%)	Average of tweets per day	Average reply rate on twitter	Times links were included in tweets	Number of tweets retweeted
King Abdullah II	33.45%	17.82%	0.13	1%	0	163
Prime Minister	6.23%	7.12%	0.67	19%	365	809
Ministry of Education	11.44%	2.19%	2.57	35%	1 054	1 604
Ministry of Health	7.05%	1.74%	1.55	3%	501	1 508
Ministry of Higher Education	3.74%	0.96%	1.7	45%	601	454
Ministry of Culture	3.21%	0.02%	0.6	0	1 073	82
Social Security Corporation	2.44%	0.03%	0.94	11%	292	300
Ministry of Labor	2.04%	0.08%	0.96	0	2 066	302
JIC	1.23%	0.08%	1.18	7%	837	995
Ministry of Tourism	0.62%	0.35%	2.33	4%	606	1 171
Ministry of Entrepreneurship and Digital Economy	0.59%	0.41%	2.26	12%	661	1 419
Ministry of Trade and Industry	0.55%	0.03%	1.48	1%	153	44
Ministry of Awqaf and Religious Affairs	0.52%	0.08%	0.8	7%	1 183	591
Minister of State for Media Affairs	0.49%	1.82%	6.79	16%	180	2 055
Ministry of Justice	0.38%	0.26%	0.71	2%	1 158	632
MoPIC	0.27%	0.30%	2.21	5%	1 248	1 356
Ministry of Transport	0.06%	0.00%	-	-	-	-

Note: Analysis of all tweets emitted by each institutional account from September 2020 – October 2020.
Source: Author's calculations using twitonomy and World Bank Population data from 2019.

Without a standardised framework or guidance, however, the use of social media will not harness its full potential as a means to promote engagement. MoSMA could consider formalising and sharing more widely the series of internal standard operating procedures outlining the do's and don'ts it has developed (see Box 4.3 for examples of related guidelines). MoSMA could also encourage the inclusion of specific objectives and evaluation indicators in communication plans to regularly measure social media performance. Another means of encouraging an interactive use of social media is clarifying, harmonising and simplifying validation protocols for posting and responding on social media. The use of guidelines in this regard is a common practice in OECD countries to mitigate the risks presented by these platforms. For their success, future efforts should be co-ordinated as part of the country's broader digital transformation agenda.

> **Box 4.3. Examples of social media guidelines in OECD countries**
>
> **Norway**
>
> The Norwegian Digitalisation Agency's comprehensive social media guidance for public administration (available online) refers to a wide range of legal provisions and regulations such as the Ethical guidelines for the civil service, the Human Rights Act, and the Personal Data Act. While outlining the ways in which social media can be used, the guidelines also include potential risks, such as viral spread of content, ownership of content, and privacy implications. The guidance also includes directives on archiving and clearly specifies the roles and responsibilities of the various actors of the public sphere, from the Minister to the head of department, to the communicator. This is also supplemented with the importance of distinguishing between individual (i.e. personal) and public servant accounts.
>
> **Colombia**
>
> The Presidential Advisory of Communications in Colombia's succinct social media guideline outlines the benefits of social media use in the context of government, the qualities and characteristics that are required for effective content, including security, content validation, interactivity, and ethical principles. The guidelines also caution against disinformation, by providing a few questions that one must ask him/herself to prevent the spread of false or harmful information. Complementing these directives, the Government of Colombia issued a series of protocols for online interactivity with the public in social media platforms
>
> **Chile**
>
> The Government of Chile's Digital Kit is a one-stop-shop where public communicators can consult manuals, tools and templates to facilitate their daily work on social media. These resources include manuals on managing institutional websites, applying graphic norms for government visual material, ensuring inclusive communication free of gender stereotypes and social media use in general. The platform also provides templates for websites, typographies and a library of visual material to align the communication of all ministries under one visual identity and narrative.
>
> As part of the resources therein, the portal houses the government-wide social media guidance document ("*Decálogo de Comunicación en Redes Sociales para Cuentas Gubernamentales*"). The guideline provides a series of recommendations for different types of government accounts on generating effective content, managing interactions with users and defining the role of community managers. The document also includes concrete information on: the overall communication objectives of the National Administration; Engaging with the public Designing effective visual and audio content for different audiences; Managing crisis communication through social media; Developing a digital content strategy; Monitoring and evaluation mechanisms; and Addressing privacy and security concerns.
>
> Source: Author's own work, based on OECD (2021[7]); http://www.gobiernoenredes.gov.co/protocolo-interaccion-redes-sociales/; https://www.difi.no/fagomrader-og-tjenester/klart-sprak-og-brukerinvolvering/sosiale-medier/veiledning-i-sosiale-medier; https://kitdigital.gob.cl/

The Government of Jordan could also explore collaborations with influencers, civil society and the private sector to increase the reach of specific communication activities online. With the exception of partnerships with the media, OECD evidence suggests this is not a common practice across ministries (see Figure 4.4). Nonetheless, trends reveal that influencer content has significantly affected media consumption patterns in the country. According to the *2019 Media Use Report in the Middle East*, more than 57% of Jordanians look at influencer posts, 18% tend to adopt their commercial recommendations, and 23% obtain news from these actors (Northwestern University, 2019[8]). In the context of the COVID-19 crisis, many countries including Finland and Switzerland for instance, collaborated with influencers to promote the adoption of emergency health measures(see Box 4.4).

Figure 4.4. Share of Jordanian Ministries partnering with the below stakeholders to boost the reach of digital communication activities

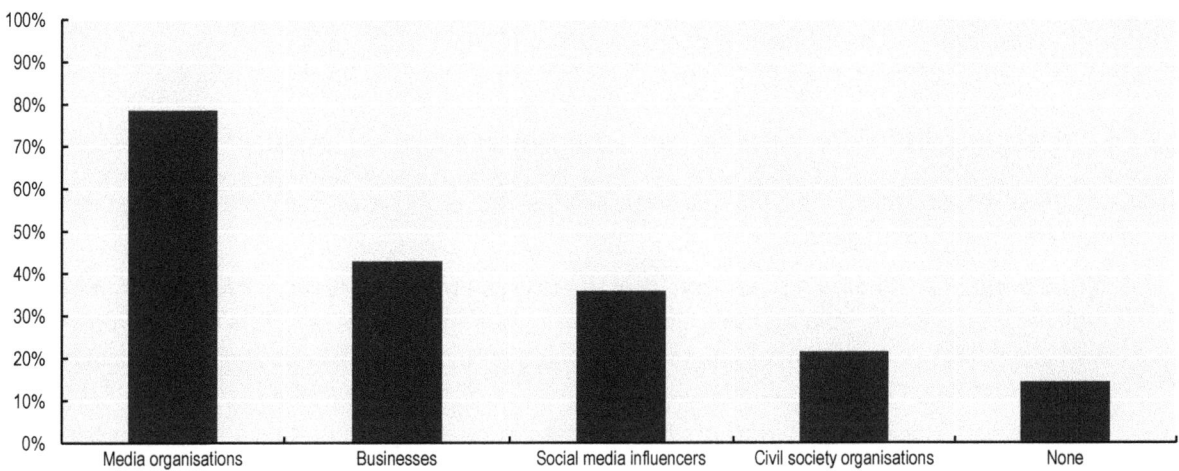

Note: N=14, responses to the question: "With which of the following stakeholders, if any, (either paid for or in-kind/free) does the institution partner with in order to boost the reach of its digital communications".
Source: OECD (2020), Survey for ministries in Jordan: Understanding public communication in Jordan.

Box 4.4. Partnering with trusted voices to expand the reach of communication online

Finland

The Prime Minister's Office of Finland, in collaboration with the National Emergency Supply Agency, PING Helsinki and Mediapool, partnered with social media influencers to provide lifesaving information for younger segments of the population, which can be harder to reach through traditional means. Following a thorough influencer mapping, over 1 800 Finnish figures helped the government share clear, up to date and relevant information on health measures. A follow-up survey conducted by PING Helsinki revealed that "94% of followers felt they got enough information and instructions about coronavirus via influencers with over half saying influencer communication affected their behaviour" and "97% of respondents consider the COVID-19 information shared by influencers reliable".

Switzerland

Led by the head of the Federal Department of Home Affairs, the Government of Switzerland launched the #soschützenwiruns ("this is how we protect ourselves") campaign, where influencers shared images and videos to educate audiences that staying home helps protect vulnerable groups and reduces the strain on the healthcare system. The Government partnered with these popular figures by providing relevant communication material to help disseminate.

Sources: OECD (2020[2]), *Building resilience to the COVID-19 pandemic: The role of centres of government*; OECD (2021[9]), *Enhancing public trust in COVID-19 vaccination: The role of governments*.

Evaluating the impact of public communication

Evaluation mechanisms are one of the main building blocks of a strategic public communication approach and refers to "the systematic and objective measurement of an ongoing or completed project, programme or policy, its design, implementation and results" (OECD, 2009[10]) (see Box 4.5). Evaluation can be a critical tool to ensure that initiatives (i.e. campaigns, social media posts, etc.) reach their desired goals, by linking messages, audiences and outcomes with changes in behaviour and broader policy objectives. This practice can also reinforce accountability and learning feedback loops for the deployment of more evidence-driven policies and their effective communication (OECD, 2020[11]).

Box 4.5. Conceptual distinction between monitoring, measuring, and evaluating policies

For the purpose of this report, the OECD distinguishes the process of monitoring, measuring, and evaluating with the following definitions:

- **Monitoring:** "A continuing function that uses systematic collection of data on specified indicators to provide management and the main stakeholders of an ongoing [...] intervention with indications of the extent of progress and achievement of objectives and progress in the use of allocated funds" (OECD, 2009[12]).
- **Measuring:** "The collection and analysis of data in relation to a particular object, process, or condition (Macnamara, 2018)".
- **Evaluating:** "The systematic and objective assessment of an ongoing or completed project, programme or policy, its design, implementation, and results. The aim is to determine the relevance and fulfilment of objectives, [...] efficiency, effectiveness, impact, and sustainability. An evaluation should provide information that is credible and useful, enabling the incorporation of lessons learned into the decision-making process of both recipients and donors. Evaluation also refers to the process of determining the worth or significance of an activity, policy, or programme (OECD, 2009[12])".

Source: Based on (OECD, 2009[12]), "OECD DAC Glossary" in *Guidelines for Project and Programme Evaluations*, OECD, Paris, www.oecd.org/development/evaluation/dcdndep/47069197.pdf; Macnamara (2018[13]), *Evaluating Public Communication: Exploring new Models, Standards and Best Practice.*

Institutionalising evaluation enables central communication teams to measure performance in a consistent manner, as well as ensure the efficient allocation and use of resources. It "can contribute to improving the comparability and consistency of results across time, institutions, and disciplines, allowing the continuity of data interpretation (OECD, 2020[11])". Doing so may underline the value of public communication and make the business case for further investments in this function, in addition to enabling accountability and learning to better inform future policy.

Nonetheless, the practice of evaluating public communication remains underutilised in a large share of countries (OECD, 2021[7]) Despite a wide diversity of contexts, Macnamara (2020[14]) argues that the difficulty of moving from theory to practice inhibits progress in this area, and experts have failed to achieve consensus on the best instruments and methods to evaluate public communication. Other challenges impeding the proper use of evaluations in this field range from those of an operational to a technical nature within Government (Macnamara, 2020[14]) (Luoma-aho and Canel, 2020[15]).[2]

These challenges are no different in Jordan, where the lack of an institutionalised methodology has inhibited media units from fully leveraging the benefits of evaluating public communication. As Figure 4.5 illustrates, such initiatives are carried out on an ad hoc basis, if conducted at all, by two thirds of responding ministries. This is also the case for MoSMA, where there is no person or unit institutionally charged with this task. OECD data furthermore revealed that existing evaluations primarily focus on measuring the reach of digital communication through social media monitoring, which on its own is not sufficient to effectively inform policy.

Figure 4.5. Average frequency of the evaluation of public communication competencies by ministries in Jordan

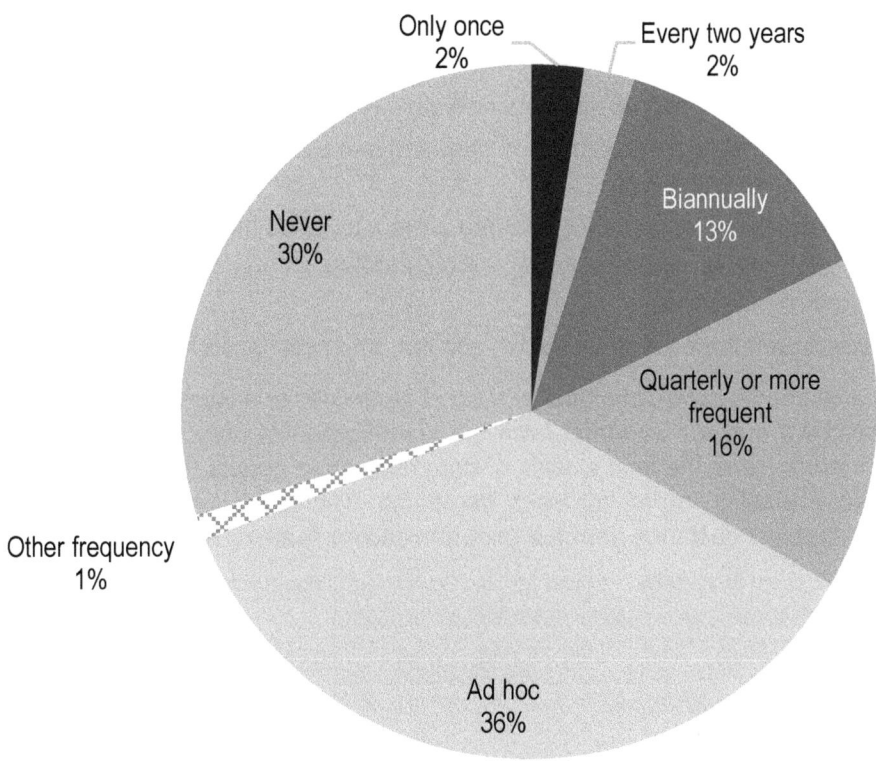

Note: N=14, average frequency of responses to the question: "How often, if at all, is the impact of the following institution communication functions evaluated?".
Source: OECD (2020), Survey for ministries in Jordan: Understanding public communication in Jordan.

For evaluations to reach their desired objectives, the Government of Jordan could consolidate existing practices by linking evaluation metrics with broader organisational and policy goals. OECD survey results revealed that a majority of ministries report the existence of evaluation metrics and key performance indicators for public communication activities. Nonetheless, findings from validation workshops note that such metrics are not always used, with staff often lacking skills for this purpose. Moreover, interviews with stakeholders revealed challenges in measuring the impact of public communication activities; for example, going beyond the measurement of outputs or outcomes. Measuring changes in stakeholder participation levels, behaviour change, and evolutions in the uptake of public services could be an important step in this regard.

To this end, the Government of Jordan could consider the creation of a central entity in charge of overseeing communication evaluations across government, given the technical nature of this task. As a first step to institutionalising procedures across public institutions, the impact evaluation guide from the Department of Institutional Development at the PMO could be customised to the needs of public communicators. To ensure successful implementation, the Government of Jordan could consider building technical capabilities within ministries to ground evaluations in user-driven and robust evidence-based approaches to showcase impact, as done in the Government of New South Wales in Australia (see Box 4.6).

> **Box 4.6. Evaluation framework of the government of New South Wales in Australia**
>
> The evaluation framework from the Government of New South Wales seeks to ensure the delivery of effective public communication by clarifying objectives, identifying different audiences and measuring the impact of activities through an institutionalised approach. The Framework - together with a matrix mapping evaluation feedback loops on inputs, activities, outputs, outcomes and impact – sets out a coherent approach to evaluating public communication under the following principles:
>
> - Set SMART communication objectives and align with government and organisational goals.
> - Adopt a "programme logic" approach to planning and evaluation by identifying inputs, activities, outputs, outcomes and impact.
> - Incorporate feedback loops throughout the project to refine the strategy and adjust tactics.
> - Consider the needs and concerns of stakeholders and the community when setting communication objectives.
> - Take into account the economic, social, cultural, and political context.
>
> The framework is moreover complemented by a set of guidelines to ensure its effective implementation. The guiding document outlines 20 steps from the identification of objectives, to the selection of the evaluation methodology and the final stages of communicating results through the development and submission of an evaluation report for each campaign. Technical support for public authorities is complemented with direct guidance from the communications team of NSW.
>
> Source: Author's own work, based on the below resources from the Government of New South Wales:
> Evaluation framework template: https://www.nsw.gov.au/sites/default/files/2020-03/NSW%20Government%20evaluation%20framework%20for%20advertising%20and%20communications_0.pdf
> Evaluation Matrix: Implementation Guidelines: https://www.nsw.gov.au/sites/default/files/2020-03/Guidelines%20for%20Implementing%20the%20NSW%20Government%20Evaluation%20Framework.pdf

Recommendations

This chapter identified avenues to strengthen core competencies within public institutions. It underlined the importance of leveraging audience insights, digital communication and impact evaluation in support of increased transparency, integrity, accountability and stakeholder participation through the work of communicators.

Utilising audience insights to better link concepts, messages, and channels with the needs and expectations of citizens

- Ensure that the selection of key messages, channels and visual aids respond to the needs, habits, and expectations of different segments of the population, at both the national and local level. Special attention should be given to tailoring communication for vulnerable or marginalised segments of the population - such as women, youth, and refugees among others.
- Continue the professionalisation efforts underway for the use of audience insights across ministries in Jordan by formally including it as a mandatory task for all media units and providing related training.
- Consider the creation of a central hub within the PMO to monitor, collect insights from different audiences and share it across the administration.

Leveraging the interactivity benefits of digital communication

- Build internal capabilities to leverage the interactivity benefits of online platforms. This could take form of specialised trainings or the creation of dedicated communities of practice to share good practices on issues such as social media use, data analytics, web presence, etc.
- Ensure institutional websites and Facebook pages are up to date, provide easy access to information and centralise relevant documents such as calendars of events, policy documents and other project statistics.
- Communicate regularly about available consultation opportunities and make use of digital platforms, beyond just social media, to crowdsource relevant contributions from the public and establish online spaces for dialogue on key policy issues.
- Develop whole-of-government social media guidelines including for the management of institutional accounts, personal profiles of public officials and online stakeholder participation.
- Encourage collaboration with influencers, civil society and businesses to expand the scale and reach of digital communication campaigns, in particular for younger segments of the population.

Evaluating the impact of public communication

- Institutionalise evaluations through a whole-of-government framework with clear processes, methods, metrics, timelines, and reporting mechanisms. Such a framework could build on the impact evaluation guide from the Department of Institutional Development at the PMO and be customised to the needs of media units. Specific output, outcome, and impact metrics can be identified in this framework, including for instance changes in behaviours, in levels of stakeholder participation or in the take up of public services.
- Build technical capabilities within ministries to ground evaluations in user-driven and evidence-based approaches to inform future endeavours and policies.
- Consider the creation of a central entity in charge of overseeing the evaluation of public communication, given the highly technical nature of this task and providing trainings when needed.

References

Communications Community Office of Canada (2019), *Annual Report (2019-2020)*, https://www.canada.ca/en/privy-council/services/communications-community-office/reports/annual-2019-2020.html#toc5. [4]

Kemp, S. (2020), *Digital 2020: Jordan*, https://datareportal.com/reports/digital-2020-jordan. [5]

Luoma-aho, V. and M. Canel (eds.) (2020), *The Handbook of Public Sector Communication*, Wiley, http://dx.doi.org/10.1002/9781119263203. [15]

Macnamara, J. (2020), *New Developments in Best Practice Evaluation*, Wiley, http://dx.doi.org/10.1002/9781119263203.ch28. [14]

Macnamara, J. (2018), *Evaluating Public Communication: Exploring new Models, Standards and Best Practice*. [13]

Murphy, K. (2019), *Government Communications in a Digital Age*, Nomos Verlagsgesellschaft mbH & Co. KG, http://dx.doi.org/10.5771/9783845298030. [3]

Northwestern University (2019), *2019 Media use in the Middle East*, https://www.qatar.northwestern.edu/news/articles/NUQ_Media_Use_2019.pdf. [8]

OECD (2021), "Enhancing public trust in COVID-19 vaccination: The role of governments", *OECD Policy Responses to Coronavirus (COVID-19)*, OECD Publishing, Paris, https://doi.org/10.1787/eae0ec5a-en. [9]

OECD (2021), *OECD Report on Public Communication: The Global Context and the Way Forward*, OECD Publishing, Paris, https://doi.org/10.1787/22f8031c-en. [7]

OECD (2020), *Building resilience to the Covid-19 pandemic: the role of centres of government*, http://www.oecd.org/coronavirus/policy-responses/building-resilience-to-the-covid-19-pandemic-the-role-of-centres-of-government-883d2961/. [2]

OECD (2020), *Engaging Citizens in Jordan's Local Government Needs Assessment Process*, OECD Public Governance Reviews, OECD Publishing, Paris, https://dx.doi.org/10.1787/c3bddbcb-en. [6]

OECD (2020), *Improving Governance with Policy Evaluation: Lessons From Country Experiences*, OECD Public Governance Reviews, OECD Publishing, Paris, https://dx.doi.org/10.1787/89b1577d-en. [11]

OECD (2020), *OECD Centre of Government Survey 2020: Understanding Public Communication*. [1]

OECD (2009), *Guidelines for Project and Programme Evaluations*, https://www.oecd.org/development/evaluation/dcdndep/47069197.pdf. [10]

OECD (2009), "OECD DAC Glossary", in *Guidelines for Project and Programme Evaluations*, OECD, Paris, http://www.oecd.org/development/evaluation/dcdndep/47069197.pdf. [12]

Notes

[1] Vulnerable segments which public communication activities seek to target: Youth (aged 15 to 29) (57%); People with special needs or disabilities (43%); Women (43%); Middle-aged individuals (40 to 60 years) (36%); Ethnic minorities (36%); No specific groups targeted (21%); Low income groups (21%); The elderly (people aged 65+) (21%); Refugees (14%); Non-native language speakers (7%); Groups in specific regions of the country (7%).

[2] On the one hand, operational limitations underline the lack of research, knowledge and skills, disciplinary siloes within public entities and conceptual misunderstanding between monitoring and evaluating activities (Macnamara, 2020[14]; Luoma-aho and Canel, 2020[15]). On the other, a focus on output indicators, reliance on biases and assumptions, the measurement of intangibles and the lack of formative (ex-ante) evaluations are hindering the implementation of this function (ibid).

5 Leveraging the media and information ecosystem in Jordan

This chapter seeks to assess Jordan's media and information enabling environment in order to determine how it can be best leveraged in support of its ongoing public communication and media engagement efforts. With a focus to improving media and information ecosystems, the analysis seeks to evaluate a number of political economy issues from structural, institutional, and stakeholder perspectives, including critical gaps and challenges that exist. Accordingly, this chapter will provide targeted recommendations to address the challenges identified and help the government of Jordan to best utilise the media to communicate its public policy priorities.

A robust and well-regulated media and information enabling environment is vitally important to how Jordan communicates around a variety of pertinent public policy priorities, including its response to the COVID-19 pandemic; the government's larger public sector reform initiatives; as well as its Open Government reform agenda and the upcoming consultation process for the development of the 5th Open Government Partnership (OGP) National Action Plan (NAP). In order to assess the potential role that media as well as the larger enabling environment can play in the public policy process, it is necessary to understand: (i) key structural and contextual dimensions, including historical, political, macroeconomic, and sociocultural issues that impact public communications and the media; (ii) key laws and institutions, including de jure/de facto legal frameworks, regulations, and institutional arrangements that impact public communication and the media; as well as (iii) key stakeholder dynamics of the actors involved in the media, including their incentives, financial resources, and human resource capacities, all of which can greatly impact the role of public communications and the media.

Structural issues affecting access to media and information

The first part of the analysis seeks to analyse the government's ability to effectively leverage public communications and engage with media to deliver key messages with respect to the various structural constraints that may exist. In particular, this section considers a number of structural issues that can have a binding effect on access to media and information, including: (i) geographic and infrastructure determinants, such as penetration of broadband internet, cell phone technologies, and satellite access across the territory; (ii) socio-economic determinants, including the existence of a digital divide in the population on the basis of income, gender, or age; as well as (iii) exogenous or geopolitical determinants, such as how the global COVID pandemic and conflicts in neighbouring countries can affect the production, consumption, and engagement with the media.

Infrastructure and spatial challenges

Over the period considered, available evidence suggests that Jordan has made notable progress in terms of access and availability of media transmitted through print, broadcast, mobile, and online channels. Based on improvements to Jordan's ICT infrastructure, now more than 8.7 million Jordanians have access to mobile subscriptions and 9.1 million Jordanians to the internet (TRA, 2019[1]). When disaggregated between fixed and broadband internet connections, the data suggests that a majority of Jordanians access internet data through their smartphones, as has been confirmed by recent Telecommunication Development Indicators: "95.6% of all internet subscriptions were mobile broadband subscriptions at the end of 2018, with the number of fixed-line subscriptions steadily decreasing" (Ibid). These figures are confirmed by the most recent World Development Indicators, which note that 77% of Jordanians have access to mobile phones and 66% use the internet, while currently only 4.6% of Jordanians access information through fixed broadband subscriptions and 3.5% through fixed telephone subscriptions (see Figure 5.1) (World Bank, 2019[2]). Finally, access to television broadcast has likewise grown, with a satellite penetration rate reaching 90% of households providing access to regional and global news providers (UNESCO, 2015[3]).

Figure 5.1. Core ICT indicators in Jordan 2010-19

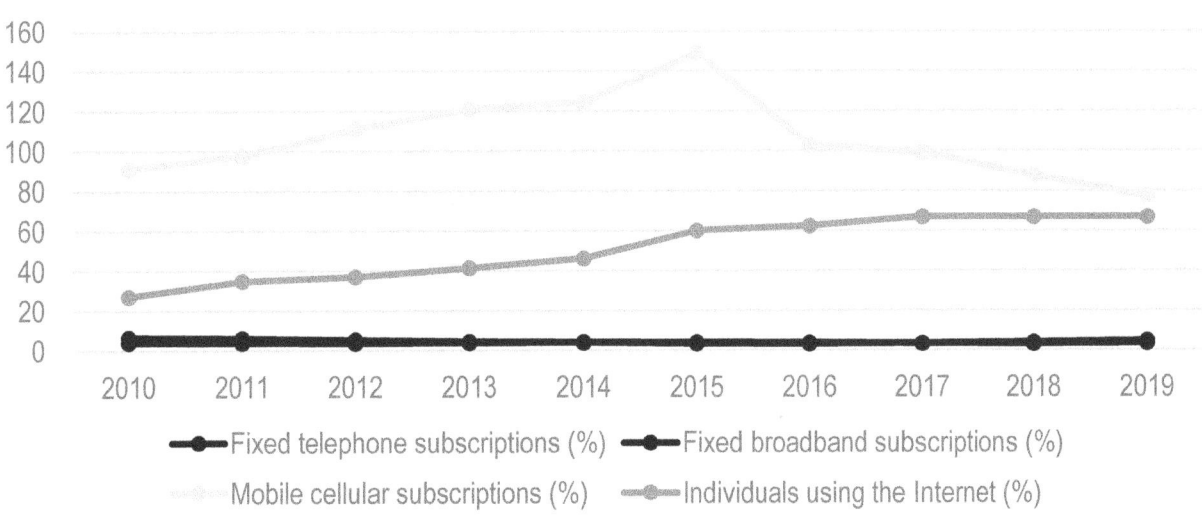

Source: World Development Indicators, 2010-2019.

Despite the growth of mobile and fixed broadband subscribers, geography and population distribution continues to limit access to the media and information across the territory. Based on the 2015 Jordan Population and Housing census, the overall population in Jordan consists of approximately 9.5 million individuals, of which a third are non-Jordanians. The population, however, is unevenly distributed across governorates, with 75% of all inhabitants concentrated in Amman (4 million), Irbid (1.77 million) and Zarqa (1.36 million) respectively (The Kingdom of Jordan's Department of Statistics, 2019[4]) (OECD, 2020[5]) (OECD, 2017[6]). As illustrated by Figure 5.2, broadband internet continues to have a lower penetration rate in territories outside of main urban centres such as Amman, which may limit media and information consumption from social media and online outlets in these places. At the same time, while more than 82% of Jordanians consumed news primarily via television, radio has been noted as the second most popular news source for Jordanians, particularly for those in rural areas who do not have access to internet or satellite technologies (Fanack, 2019[7]). Traditional print media can likewise suffer from distribution challenges across the country, particularly in remote areas; however, it should be noted that even in 2011, less than 3% of Jordanians primarily access the news via newspapers (Ibid).

Figure 5.2. Internet access by sub-districts, 2010-16

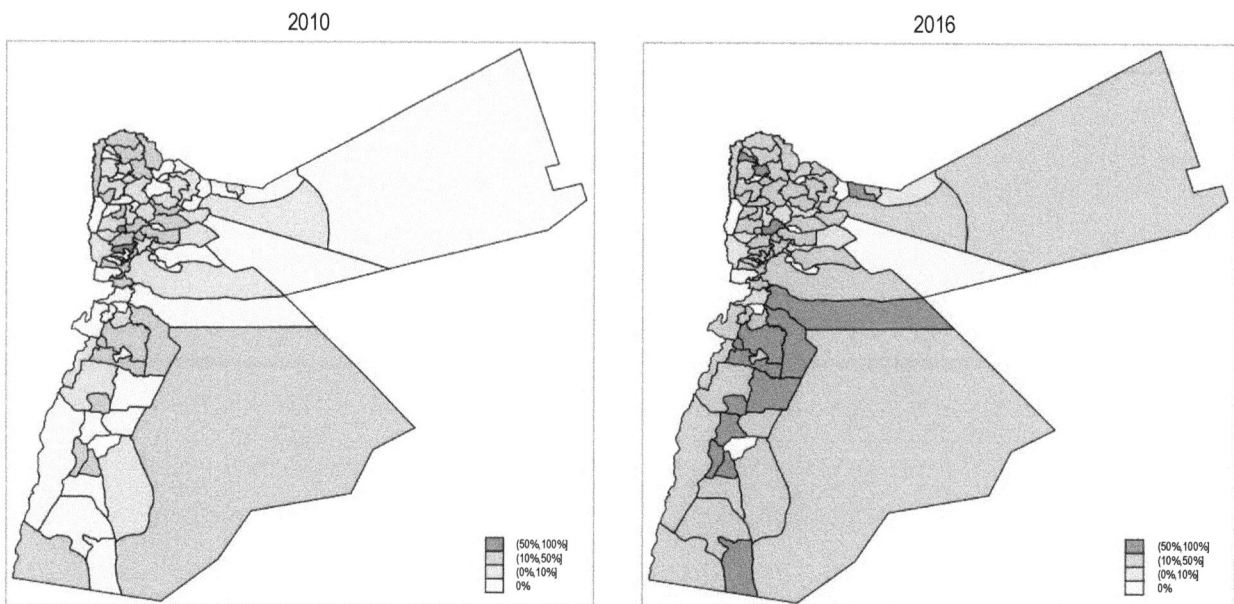

Source: World Bank (2020[8]), Does the internet reduce gender gaps? The case of Jordan, available online at http://documents1.worldbank.org/curated/en/282451584107082621/pdf/Does-the-Internet-Reduce-Gender-Gaps-The-Case-of-Jordan.pdf

Further exacerbating the unequal use and access of broadcast technologies that support media and information, additional geographic challenges exist which may affect the salience of news stories across the territory. To be sure, most media outlets tend to be concentrated in the capital, Amman, with less coverage of issues and new stories occurring in the various governorates. In meetings with civil society and media experts, participants have confirmed this trend, suggesting that there is little media coverage of issues outside of Amman aside from high-level visits, events, or "ribbon-cutting" ceremonies. In order to cope with uneven access to media and information via television and internet as well as uneven coverage of local events by traditional news sources, OECD survey results indicate a clear preference by local authorities to use social media (72%) and formal communication methods (62%), including the use of official government letters to communicate with local audiences (OECD, 2020[5]).

Demographic and distributional challenges

In addition to the geographic disparities noted above, a growing "digital divide" has emerged as an additional cross-cutting structural issue in Jordan, which makes equal access to media and information platforms difficult to fully achieve. In this regard, a digital divide can be viewed as "the unequal access of citizens to information and communication technology (ICT), and unequal possession of the skills and experiences needed to optimise this technology that keeps people from taking advantage of public services through the Internet or other ICT channels (Abu-Shanab and Al-Jamal, 2015[9]). As will be described below, evidence suggests the existence of such a "digital divide" between key segments of the population in Jordan.

A first element of the digital divide can be linked to income and income distribution across segments of the population, which may impact both the opportunities and means to access media and information. In particular, official statistics suggest that around 15.7% of the population in the country live in extreme poverty (The Kingdom of Jordan's Department of Statistics, 2019[4]) (Middle East Monitor, 2019[10]). These measures of poverty have been put into even further relief based on the economic impacts of the Coronavirus (COVID-19) pandemic, whereby the World Bank estimates suggest that poverty rates may increase by up to 21.6% as additional households are pushed over the poverty line (defined as USD 1.90 per day in 2011 PPP) (World Bank, 2021[11]).

As noted above, these income dynamics are further exaggerated when taking into account the distribution of spatial poverty across the country, including income disparities that persist across Governorates and between urban and rural communities (OECD, 2020[5]). According to the Kingdom of Jordan's Department of Statistics (2019[4]), Amman is home to "over 40% of the total population, with more than half of all households in the country (59%) in 2018 falling into high or upper-middle-income segments". Nevertheless, when disaggregated by region, the "North appears to have the highest number of low-income households (29%) compared to the Central (15%) and Southern (23%) regions. Government data also found that a majority of the population in Madaba (61%), Mafraq (75%), Jarash (59%), Ajloun (55%), Tafiela (57%), and Ma'an (60%) fall in the lowest income quantiles" (see Figure 5.3) (ibid).

Figure 5.3. Household income by quintile

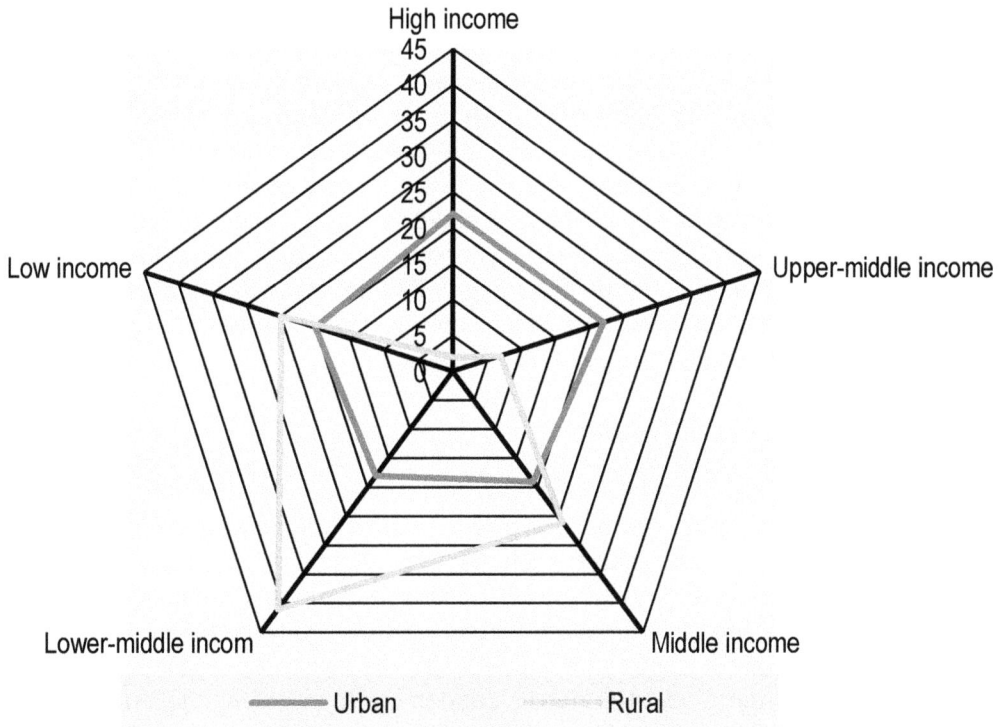

Source: The Kingdom of Jordan's Department of Statistics (2019[4]), Jordan Population and Family Health Survey 2017-18, https://www.dhsprogram.com/pubs/pdf/FR346/FR346.pdf

Based on these spatial poverty dynamics, it is perhaps not surprising that those in areas with a higher incidence of household poverty may have less access to the channels that provide media coverage and information, especially satellite and internet-enabled channels. This is driven by the fact that mobile internet in Jordan is taxed at comparatively high levels, thus amounting to a barrier to broadband access, particularly for the poor (GSMA, 2018[12]). Moreover, data suggests that taxes placed on telecom services, and internet services, in particular, have increased over the period, from 8% to 16% in 2017 (Jordan Times, 2018[13]). Based on the Jordan Department of Statistics survey (2019[4]), "10.5% of respondents cited high costs as a reason for not accessing the internet, up from 8.5% in 2016". In addition, the same survey suggested that "cost impedes access more in rural areas, where 17.3% of residents do not access the internet due to the price of service, compared to 9.5% in urban areas" (ibid). Similarly, recent results by the

Pew Research Centre suggest that internet and smartphone usage is 80% for high-income households but only 50% for low-income households (Silver et al., 2019[14]).

In addition to disparities in income across regions in Jordan, gender is another element that can contribute to a digital divide. To be sure, a number of statistics suggest that women may not enjoy the same access to media and information as men. In particular, survey data collected by a 2018 Pew Research Centre study found that women lag men in a number of key indicators, including internet use (89% for men 84% for women), smartphone use (86% for men 83% for women), social media platform and messaging app use (85% for men 78% for women), and Facebook use (80% for men 61% for women) (Silver et al., 2019[14]). In a recent study evaluating men's perceptions of women having equal access to broadband internet connections and computers, survey data indicates that "a total of 43.9% of educated men were opposed to women using computers with the Internet [and] only a meagre 26% of men were fully in favour of women using the Internet" (Abu-Shanab and Al-Jamal, 2015[9]).

A final structural element that can contribute to the digital divide is based on age and levels of education, with a bulge in young educated Jordanians having greater access to the technologies that allow them to connect with media and information platforms. Jordan is one of the youngest countries in the world, with more than one-third of the population aged between 12-30 years (OECD, 2020[5]). According to the Pew Research Centre, there is a "real and pervasive" demographic divide among internet users in Jordan. The youth (defined as those between 1-14 years of age) have an 18% higher use rate of internet and smart phone technologies (75% in total) in comparison with the over-40 demographic (57% in total) (Poushter, 2016[15]). Given the number of highly educated young Jordanians and recent graduates, this digital divide is even further reinforced. In particular, survey data collected by a subsequent 2018 Pew Research Centre study found that more educated individuals use technologies to access media than less educated individuals, including internet use (95% for more educated; 78% for less educated), smartphone use (93% for more educated; 76% for less educated), and social media platform and messaging app use (92% for more educated; 70% for less educated) (Silver et al., 2019[14]).

Exogenous and geopolitical challenges

A final structural element that can present challenges to Jordan's media and information environment is the role that exogenous shocks—both regional and global—can play in defining the media and information enabling environment. These include issues such as the refugee crisis perpetuated by conflicts in neighbouring countries, including a continuing civil conflict in Syria and ensuing instability in Iraq; a weakened security situation as the government of Jordan confronts terrorism, illicit arms trade, and other security threats posed by regional spill-overs; as well as the economic strains and service delivery challenges brought about by the global COVID-19 pandemic. Such global challenges can significantly impact media and information ecosystems in a number of ways, including: (i) how producers of news and media can effectively and safely operate in certain areas in their role as reporters, watchdogs, and intermediaries of information; (ii) how much access citizens have to media and information technologies in these regions; as well as (iii) the attention and salience that the government and public communicators assign to other non-priority issues given the pressing and political nature of overriding global challenges.

Over the past 15 years, massive dislocations fuelled by conflicts in Syria and Iraq have created tremendous pressures on the government to deal with an influx of refugees. In 2019, UNHCR recorded approximately 747 080 refugees in the country, with a significant share (83.5%) primarily living in urban areas (OECD, 2020[5]; UNHCR, 2020[16]) The vast majority of refugees come from Syria (654 692) and are concentrated in Jordan's most densely populated governorates, including Amman (29.5%), Mafraq (24.8%) and Irbid (20.6%) respectively (ibid). This influx has strained public service delivery and raised concerns around ensuring the long-term socio-economic integration of this group (OECD, 2020[5]).

At the same time, these challenges can significantly impact the production, consumption, and salience of issues covered by media outlets and information platforms in Jordan. With respect to media coverage, a deteriorating security situation may restrict how and when media outlets and citizen journalists are able to cover certain issues, particularly those that are of interest to national security priorities. To be sure, UN Women conducted a 2020 study that found that vulnerable groups—particularly refugee women in Jordan's Al-Azraq and Al-Za'atari camps—have limited access to enabling technologies that allow them to receive critical media coverage and information sources. In particular, the study found that less than 1% of survey respondents had access to a laptop, desktop, or tablet computer, only 43% were able to access internet through their own smartphone, although only 14% did not have a smartphone but were able to use a family member's smartphone to access the internet (UN WOMEN, 2020[17]). Such statistics point to the cross-cutting nature of the poverty, gender, and infrastructure challenges noted above—all of which greatly limit the access of the most vulnerable groups to media and information.

Exacerbating these pre-existing dynamics is the massive strain that the ongoing COVID-19 pandemic may have on the functioning of media and information ecosystems. As such, many countries in the world, and in Jordan in particular, have been forced to respond quickly to ensure the health and safety of its citizens. Linked to the refugee crisis described above, the government has co-ordinated with UNHCR to put in place measures to guarantee access to national health services for refugees (OECD, 2020[18]). With respect to media and information ecosystems, rapid government engagement can help to set the public policy agenda; identify, evaluate, and select policy options; as well as to monitor the effects of policies. All of these functions are critically relevant to the COVID-19 response, especially as governments grapple with large amounts of changing information and pressures to respond in a more effective and efficient manner (OECD, 2020[18]). As noted above, vulnerable groups may not have access to the same broadband, mobile, and satellite services enjoyed by a majority of the population, thus affecting the level of depth quality, and consistency of information that they consume.

Institutional issues affecting access to media and information

This section seeks to analyse the government's ability to effectively leverage public communications and engage with the media to deliver key messages based on the various institutional arrangements that currently exist. Accordingly, this section considers the legal framework for engagement between the state and the media, interlocutors, and other producers and consumers of media content. In this regard, key laws considered include basic constitutional protections for freedom of expression, speech, and press. To implement these effectively, this section also analyses the adequacy of existing Freedom of Information (FoI) and Access to Information (A2I) legislation as well as the broader legal and regulatory environment governing the media, including laws governing online data privacy and protection, defamation, censorship, hate-speech, secrecy, as well as dis/misinformation. Finally, this section considers the "informal institutions" that may exist in the media sector, including the potential of interference, soft-containment, "red-lines," and self-censorship. In doing so, this analysis looks at both the *de jure* legal framework and *de facto* implementation—both of which are necessary to provide the necessary preconditions for an effective and efficient media ecosystem.

Constitutional provisions

From a constitutional perspective, Jordan's legal framework puts in place the necessary protections for freedom of expression, speech, and press. Adopted in 1952 and amended in 2011, Article 15 of the Constitution (2011)[1] guarantees these fundamental freedoms, as follows:

- **15.1** "The State guarantees freedom of opinion, and every Jordanian shall be free to express his opinion by speech, in writing, or by means of photographic representation and other forms of expression, provided that such does not violate the law."
- **15.2**: "Freedom of scientific research and literary, artistic, cultural, and athletic creativity shall be ensured provided that it does not contradict with the law or the public order or moral."

In addition to the protections of these freedoms, Article 15 of the 2011 constitution also provides a number of limitations and exceptions to these freedoms, as follows:

- **15.3:** "Freedom of the press, printing, publications and media shall be ensured within the limits of the law."
- **15.4:** "Newspapers shall not be suspended from publication nor shall their permits be revoked except by a judicial order and in accordance with the provisions of the law."
- **15.5:** "In case of declaration of martial law or state of emergency, it is permissible that the law imposes limited censorship on newspapers and publications, books, media and communication in matters related to public safety and national defence purposes."
- **15.6** "The law shall specify means of censorship on the resources of newspapers."

In addition to these constitutional provisions, Jordan has also ratified a number of international legal instruments that likewise support freedom of expression, speech, and press. Jordan is a signatory to the *Universal Declaration of Human Rights*[2] as well as the *International Covenant on Civil and Political Rights*.[3] Both of these seminal international legal instruments guarantee freedom of expression and opinion at the highest level within the international community. At a regional level, Jordan is a signatory to the *Arab Charter of Human Rights*.[4] Article 32 of this instrument states that "this Charter guarantees the right to information and freedom of opinion and expression, as well as the right to search for, receive, and distribute information through any means, without any consideration of geographic borders." In addition, Jordan is a signatory to other international and regional covenants that protect the core rights of freedom of expression, including the *Convention on the Rights of the Child*,[5] the *Euro-Mediterranean Association Agreement*,[6] and the *Sana'a Declaration on Promoting Independent and Pluralistic Arab Media*.[7]

Despite these international commitments and aforementioned constitutional protections, there are a number of important limitations and exceptions that may curtail these freedoms. First, as highlighted above, the 2011 Constitution includes provisions for situations when the law may legitimately place limitations on the enshrined rights, particularly in cases related to national security and cases of emergency (e.g. Article 15.5). Likewise, the Constitution includes provisions whereby subsequent legislation and/or judicial decisions may further limit the protection provided by the Constitution, including for instance, means of censorship on the press (Article 15.6). Additionally, it should be noted that the protections put forth in the 2011 Constitution only extend to Jordanians, which leaves open a large category of individuals who are not citizens, and thus not holders of these rights. This is particularly relevant given the prominence of international media outlets that operate in Jordan, as well as the large displaced populations on non-Jordanians currently living in Jordan, including more than 750 000 refugees.

Access to information legislation

A second critical element for the legal framework to support a robust media and information enabling environment is the existence of legislation guaranteeing the Right to Freedom of Information. In this regard, Jordan adopted Law No. 47 of 2007 on Securing the Right to Information Access in 2007, the first of its kind in the Arab region. Article 7 of the law provides that "each Jordanian citizen has the right to obtain the information he/she requires according to the Provisions of this Law should he/she has a lawful interest or justification."[8] The current legislation provides public officials a maximum period of 30 days to respond to information requests (Article 9) and puts in place provisions for receiving complaints should a request be denied (Article 17). The law also established the Information Council, under the National Library, as the entity responsible for the implementation and enforcement of the law.

Despite the existence of the Right to Information Access law, international observers note that the legal text is vague and includes numerous exemptions. During OECD peer review interviews, stakeholders underlined a series of challenges including that: (i) it does not require the proactive publication of information; (ii) it does not contain explicit provisions on the right to reuse information, nor does it explicitly prohibit it; (iii) it provides for a large number of exceptions, which demand a very careful interpretation of its provisions; and (iv) it does not specify penalties for infringements on the right to access information. Given these deficiencies, the Global Right to Information Rating, produced by the Global Centre for Law and Democracy, scores Jordan's Law on Securing the Right to Information Access 56 out of a possible score of 150, with a global rank of 119th out of 128 countries surveyed (see Table 5.1) (Global Centre for Democracy, 2016[19]). Likewise, UNESCO's 2015 Media Development Indicator Report noted that the law "needs to be substantially revised so as to bring it into line with international standards and better national practice, and public bodies in Jordan take the appropriate steps to implement it properly" (UNESCO, 2015[3]).

Table 5.1. Global Centre for Law and Democracy: Global Right to Information Rating in Jordan

Section	Points	Maximum score
Right of access	0	6
Scope	26	30
Requesting procedures	6	30
Exceptions and refusals	10	30
Appeals	9	30
Sanctions and protections	0	8
Promotional measures	5	16

Source: Global Centre for Democracy (2016[19]), RTI Rating, Jordan Report, available online at https://www.rti-rating.org/country-data/Jordan/.

In addition to challenges with the adequacy and scope of the law, the introduction of the law has not been followed by adequate implementation and enforcement. Many public agencies have yet to adopt or develop policies or mechanisms to implement the legislation, and in some cases, conflicting agency policies exist. Despite these challenges, OECD survey results suggest that a significant share of public communicators within ministries (10 out of 14 surveyed) co-ordinate with the office or person responsible for responding to ATI requests on a regular basis through meetings or other forms of interaction. Furthermore, OECD survey responses suggest that the majority of Ministries share regular information on the institution's activities, news and events as well as raise awareness around specific policy areas (see Figure 5.4). However, fewer Ministries share more technical information on partnerships, tenders and training opportunities, and only a small share communicate information around public consultation, anti-corruption policies, and public service contracts granted. While the type of information shared are relevant for promoting transparency in broad terms, they are indicative of a one-way communication focus, as opposed to a well-functioning balance between proactive disclosure and demand-driven information requests.

Figure 5.4. Documents made publically available, per ministry in Jordan

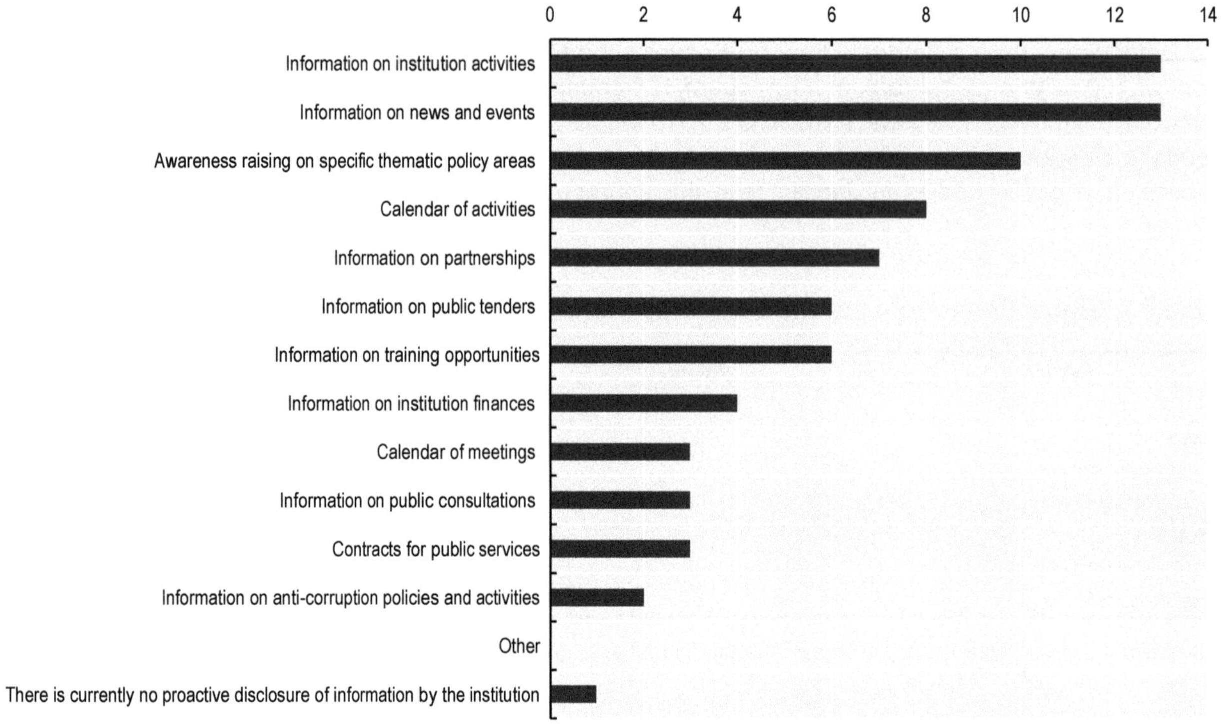

Category	Number of ministries
Information on institution activities	13
Information on news and events	13
Awareness raising on specific thematic policy areas	10
Calendar of activities	8
Information on partnerships	7
Information on public tenders	6
Information on training opportunities	6
Information on institution finances	4
Calendar of meetings	3
Information on public consultations	3
Contracts for public services	3
Information on anti-corruption policies and activities	2
Other	0
There is currently no proactive disclosure of information by the institution	1

Note: Graph depicts number of ministries, where 14 ministries responded to this question.
Source: OECD (2020), Survey for line-ministries in Jordan: Understanding public communication in Jordan.

From a demand-side perspective, the right to request information remains under-utilised by citizens, media, and CSOs. In fact, only 10 305 requests were filed by citizens between 2012 and 2015 and amounted in total to 12 101 in 2016 (OECD, 2019[20]). Findings from the OECD also noted that these challenges are exacerbated at the subnational level, where procedures to address information requests remain unclear, in particular at the level of municipalities (OECD, 2020[5]). For journalists in particular, a significant majority of those surveyed identified accessing information as a major obstacle in maintaining freedom of the press (Center for Global Communication Studies, 2011[21]).

The government of Jordan appears to have recognised many of these challenges and has been taking proactive steps to improve the implementation of the existing legislation. As noted in the country's 4th Open Government Partnership National Action Plan, the government recognises that "institutions lack a clear and uniform system for the classification and management of information [and that] the process of acquiring information by journalists and other stakeholders is characterised with difficulty and excessive bureaucracy" (Government of Jordan, 2018[22]). To address these issues, the government of Jordan developed three protocols for classifying, enforcing and managing information in late 2020 (see Box 5.1). The dissemination of these protocols, together with targeted trainings for public communicators in this regard, will be key to strengthening internal processes to manage, respond to and proactively disclose information. At the time of writing, Government counterparts noted that the Parliament was conducting a consultation with civil society on potential amendments to the 2007 ATI law.

> **Box 5.1. ATI protocols in Jordan to classify, enforce and manage information**
>
> In 2020, the Government of Jordan developed a series of protocols to strengthen the implementation of the ATI across public institutions. Their overall objective is to provide clear procedures and standards for public bodies subject to access to information law, and include the following:
>
> - **Protocol on classification** provides guidelines on how and which information should be proactively or reactively disclosed, the list of applicable exceptions, and whether a harm or a public interest test applies.
> - **Protocol for enforcement** aims to simplify the governance structures necessary for implementing the law as well as the mechanisms to strengthen internal oversight, including the preparation of annual reports and the elaboration of performance indicators.
> - **Protocol on information management** describes the procedures and technical standards for indexing documents and for building paper and electronic records.
>
> The protocols were elaborated by a multi-stakeholder committee composed of government officials, CSOs, academics, and international experts, and were subject to public consultation, and importantly, were recently adopted by the Council of Ministers in December 2020.
>
> Source: Author's own work.

Media legal and regulatory framework

In addition to the broad constitutional protections and legislation guaranteeing freedom of expression, speech, press, and access to information, it is equally important to consider how the specific media legal framework—including related laws, regulations, policies, and other institutional arrangements—can impact media and information systems. As such, this section considers the primary laws as well as the amendments or revisions that have been made over the period. Likewise, this section accounts for any regulatory requirements governing the functioning of related institutions, including the agencies responsible for overseeing print, broadcast, and online media sector as well as the behaviour of journalists. Finally, this section highlights related legislation that can affect the functioning of media and information platforms and actors, such as those related to libel, slander, defamation, blasphemy, hate speech, security, and state secrets, among others.[9]

Jordan has a complex legal framework with numerous—and sometimes overlapping—laws, directives, and regulations governing how media and broadcast organisations as well as online outlets can function. The earliest legislation comes from the Press and Publications Law (No. 8 of 1993),[10] which helped to liberalise print media, and in turn, facilitate the establishment of several private newspapers. Subsequently, the Press and Publications Law of 1998[11] introduced higher capital requirements for new media outlets and designated the Press and Publications Department[12] as the authority responsible for overseeing the sector. Concretely, this had the effect of pushing multiple independent news organisations out of business, which could not meet the new requirements (Jones, 2001[23]).

With respect to the regulatory environment, the Press Association Law (No. 15 of 1998)[13] re-established the Jordan Press Association (JPA) as responsible for regulating the journalistic profession, serving as a union for Jordanian journalists. Likewise, the Audio-visual Law (No. 71 of 2002),[14] resulted in the emergence of new radio and television stations, which considerably increased the diversity of media outlets in Jordan and established the Audio-Visual Commission (AVC) as the regulator for broadcast media (UNESCO, 2015[3]). More recently, the 1998 Press and Publications Law was amended in 2012,[15] introducing a series of requirements for news websites to obtain a government license, and applied the law's content restrictions to online publications.

In addition to these media-specific laws and regulations, there is a wide body of supporting legislation that can have a direct bearing on the media sector, including those governing online content. In this context, the 2010 Cyber Crimes Law and 2014 amendments to the Anti-Terrorism Law were their first of their kind in regulating online content, albeit with the parallel effect of restricting content online (Freedom House, 2017[24]). This initial legislation was updated on the basis of the 2015 Cybercrimes Law, which likewise has included provisions governing "illegal access (Article 3), network and information system sabotage (Article 4), unlawful interception (Article 5), credit cards and financial banking crimes (Article 6, 7, 8), pornography cybercrime (Article 9, 10), slander and denigration (Article 11), illegal reproduction of protected programme (Article 12), cyber evidence (Article 13), and involvement, intervention or incitement (Article 13)."[16] In addition to this, Jordan has a number of related laws that define libel, defamation, hate speech, blasphemy, and censorship as well as what constitute "state secrets." With respect to the laws on libel, slander, and defamation, punishments are considered criminal as opposed to civil offenses, and are severely sanctioned under the Penal Code of Jordan.

Based on the body of laws and regulations that govern media and information ecosystems, international indicators suggest a slow improvement in facilitating a free and an adequately independent environment for these sectors to function. According to the Reporters without Borders World Press Freedom Index, Jordan has improved from 143rd to 128th out of 180 countries evaluated from 2015 to 2020. On the contrary, Freedom House's Freedom of the Net Index notes a stagnation from a score of 50 out of a potential 100 in 2015 to a score of 49 out of a potential 100 in 2020. While discontinued in 2017, the Center for Protecting the Freedom of Journalists (CDFJ) produced an index measuring the status of media freedoms in Jordan that similarly indicated a low performance based on a composite index. Table 5.2 below presents a number of key metrics developed by international observers to evaluate the adequacy of Jordan's media and information enabling environment.

Table 5.2. Jordan's media and information enabling environment, 2015-20

Indicator	2015	2016	2017	2018	2019	2020
Reporters Without Borders: World Press Freedom Index Ranking ranges from 1 (most free country) to 180 (least free country)	143/180	135/180	138/180	132/180	130/180	128/180
Freedom House: Freedom of the Press Index Ranking ranges from 1 (most free country) to 180 (least free country)	145/199	145/199	150/199	XXX	XXX	XXX
Freedom House: Freedom of the Net Index Scores are based on a scale of 0 (least free) to 100 (most free)	50/100	49/100	47/100	51/100	47/100	49/100

Role of mis- and dis-information

This sub-section investigates the extent to which institutional responses to disinformation and misinformation affect the ability of the media outlets and citizen journalists to produce and disseminate information and data. In this regard, Jordan has established a disinformation platform, "Haggak Tiraf" ("You have the Right to Know"),[17] which aims to verify the information presented in news stories and social media to prevent the spread of rumours and disinformation. The platform aims to deliver information and necessary clarifications—or in the case of false or misleading information, to refute claims—in an effort to provide timely, accurate, and reliable information, and in a larger sense, to restore citizens' trust in the government. In this regard, the platform offers an "about the platform" section that presents the latest news and public interest stories; a "did you know" section that presents various national reports on different topics, awareness messages and legislative documents; as well as a fact-checking function and a video library breaking down specific rumours and other misleading or false information.

Despite the existence of the "Haggak Tiraf" platform, findings from survey validation workshops suggest that Jordan does not yet have a mature strategy, guide, or toolkit for countering mis- and dis-information, which could facilitate the objectives of the platform. Rather, survey results suggest that ministries do not follow pre-defined protocols, and those that do, rely on internal operating procedures or other ad hoc measures (see Figure 5.5). Current efforts are underway with OECD support to better understand the performance of the "Haggak Tiraf" and put in place recommendations for improvement based on international and regional good practices in countering mis- and dis-information.

Figure 5.5. Types of documents used for guiding Ministry's response to mis- anddis-information

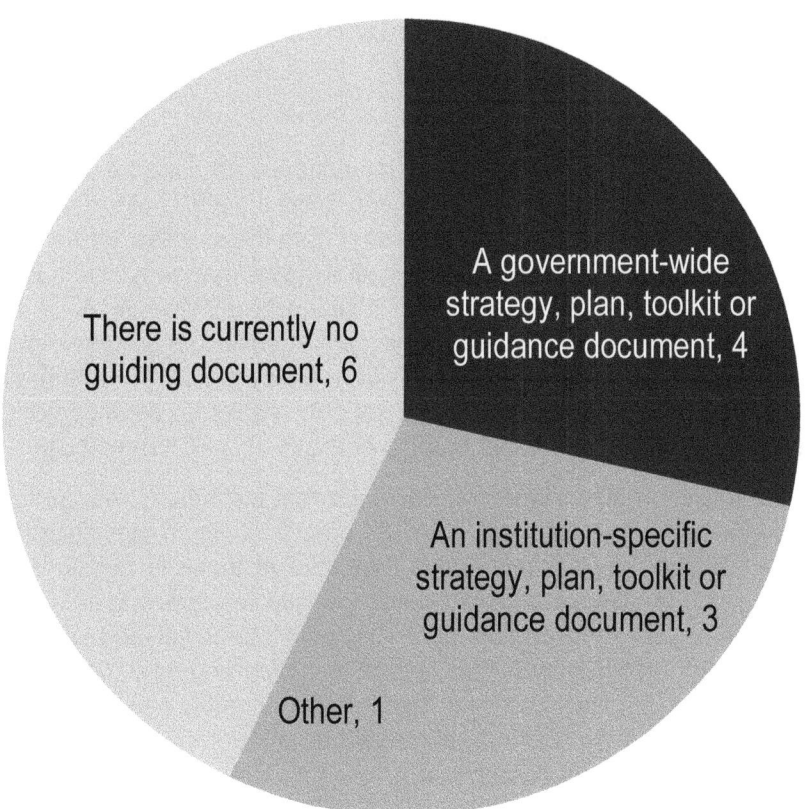

Note: The graph depicts the number of ministries. A total of 14 line ministries responded to this question.
Source: OECD (2020), Survey for line-ministries in Jordan: Understanding public communication in Jordan.

While the "Haggak Tiraf" platform has a number of useful functionalities to combat mis- and dis-information, a number of limitations likewise exist, as noted by survey respondents as well as international observers. Given the increasing flows of data and information, which have become ever more pertinent due to the ensuing COVID-19 public health crisis, a number of weaknesses have been highlighted in terms of the platform's reactivity, speed, and reach, with an overall consensus by survey respondents that mis- and dis-information responses should be deployed beyond this tool alone. For instance, the "Your Health" application and the frequent press conferences from the Prime Ministry were raised as examples, where the government can also de-bunk false information in the context of COVID-19. In addition to this, another limitation is by highlighting false content, the platform may have the unintended consequence of further publicising fake news, which would have remained otherwise unknown. This concern is shared by activists, citizens, and media outlets, some of whom "had not heard about some rumours until after the platform had published them to refute them" (Rawabdeh, 2019[25]).

In addition to challenges with the platform as a tool to counter false claims, additional institutional challenges exist with respect to how the government proactively counters mis- and dis-information. A first critical area noted by survey respondents is the lack of practical tools, skills, and mandates to identify when and how to respond to mis- and dis-information. As such, there is a growing need for government ministries and agencies to assign dedicated staff with the capacity to assess risk levels and identify rumours within ministries. Linked to this is a need for the Prime Minister's Office to proactively guide a whole-of-government approach, whereby responses to mis- and dis-information can be more strategically co-ordinated across ministries, departments, and agencies. On the demand side, additional challenges are linked to the need for regaining citizen trust in government, which as noted above, has been lagging in recent years. Accordingly, survey respondents noted how citizen trust can be further leveraged to combat false information, as well as how a lack of trust has impacted the credibility of official releases—and at times—has been taken as confirmation of the rumour itself.

Role of informal institutions

Another key political economy determinant that can influence the media and information enabling environment is the role of "informal institutions," which can affect the ability of the media to conduct its work in a free and independent manner. Importantly, these differ from the existing "formal institutions" described above, which include laws, regulations, and policies that have formal accountability and sanctioning mechanisms. However, in addition to these, "informal institutions" may emerge along the lines of traditions, societal norms, taboos, and other social practices, which are specific to a given society or culture (Helmke and Levitsky, 2004[26]; Fritz, Kaiser and Levy, 2009[27]). As noted by the OECD "informal institutions—family and kinship structures, traditions, and social norms—not only matter for development, but they are often decisive factors in shaping policy outcomes…" (Jütting et al., 2007, p. Chapter 2[28]).

With respect to media and information systems, such informal institutions may emerge around existing formal institutions, and include a number of non-codified practices, which may substitute, complement, or contradict formalised institutions. For instance, this may involve those in positions of authority utilising tactics of intimidation, threats of violence, arbitrary detention, interference, and the like. In a less draconian form, this may involve forms of "soft containment," including financial and other "in-kind" incentives provided to journalists and media outlets for favourable reporting and coverage. Finally, informal institutions may come in the form of "redlines" and "self-censorship" as journalists have an implicit knowledge of what topics or subjects not to broach—and as a result of fear of penalty or other informal consequences—decide not to report on certain topics.

With respect to informal practices of intimidation, threats of violence, arbitrary detention, or interference, evidence suggests that Jordan has improved in this regard, but further attention is needed around these issues. According to the Jordan Press Association (JPA), a number of challenges exist that affect the work of journalists, including among others, verbal and physical assaults, pressures to reveal sources of information, threats of prosecution, and summoning by security agencies (JPA, 2014[29]).[18] Likewise, the Centre for Defending the Freedom of Journalists (CDFJ) has reported issues relating to the safety of journalists, including instances of rough treatment, verbal assaults, and arbitrary dentition (CFDJ, 2011[30]). More recently, Freedom House's Freedom in the World Index 2020 notes that "gag orders and informal instructions to media outlets regarding news coverage are common [and] news websites face onerous registration requirements that, if not met, can serve as a justification for blocking" (Freedom House, 2020[31]). In most cases, international observers, including the JPA, CDFJ, Freedom House, and

UNESCO's Media Development Indicators, suggest that there is a high level of impunity for those in authority from perpetuating these acts.

Reinforcing these informal measures are forms of "soft containment" applied by those in a position of authority, which likewise jeopardise journalistic freedom and editorial independence. To be sure, survey results by the Al-Quds Centre for Political Science have cited a number of channels through which "soft containment" can be practiced, including financial grants and gifts, facilitation of procedures, access to important meetings or events, and other administrative exemptions for compliant media organisations (Jordan Media Monitor, 2012[32]). Likewise, "incentives" can likewise come from non-governmental entities, including businessmen, security forces, influential figures, CSOs, and political parties (ibid). Given these issues—which are not unique to Jordan—evidence suggests that they can have adverse effects that jeopardise journalistic independence and the content of reporting.

Finally, while there are no laws imposing prior censorship in Jordan, the informal institutions of "redlines," and relatedly, "self-censorship" are very clear. Accordingly, CDFJ survey results suggest that there are a number of topics that journalists continue to avoid criticising, representing *de facto* "redlines"—topics or subjects where journalists know they cannot tread. According to recent analytics conducted by CDFJ, key subjects that journalists "avoided" criticising include the armed forces, Royal Court, judiciary, tribal leaders, security services, and political leaders (CFDJ, 2014[33]). Likewise, journalists tend to "avoid" mentioning religious issues, sexual issues, and security issues, for fear of informal repercussion (ibid). Given these redlines, journalists engage in "self-censorship," which may be in response to wide-ranging provisions on what constitutes libel, slander, defamation, or blasphemy. As a result of this level of self-censorship, the media and information environment may not be able to function as freely as necessary to provide timely, accurate, and unbiased reporting.

Stakeholder issues affecting access to media and information

This final part of the analysis seeks to analyse the various stakeholder constraints that may exist in effectively leveraging media and information outlets to support public communication. A first element of this includes understanding *who* the stakeholders are and *how* they operate in the media ecosystem, including the roles of media producers, media consumers, media regulators, government spokespeople, as well as the CSOs and other info-mediaries who help to interpret information and make it salient for selected target audiences. To better understand the political economy dynamics between these stakeholder groups, this section seeks to explore the binding constraints, incentives, financial resources, and HR capacities that may impact the integrity of a robust media and information sector in Jordan.

Private and public media outlets

Jordan's print, broadcast, radio, and online outlets are relatively diverse, and have increased over time due to liberalised laws and fewer regulatory restrictions. While this analysis does not seek to provide a comprehensive account of all media outlets that operate in Jordan, key private and public media outlets include 21 press institutions—nine daily, nine weekly, and three monthly newspapers—as well as 139 to 141 online news websites that have been granted licenses (Al Mamlaka, 2021[34]). As noted by UNESCO, there are a number of major Arabic dailies, including Ad Dustour, Al Ghad and Al Rai, which each have a circulation in excess of 50 000, while As Sabeel,[19] Al Diyar, Al Anbat, and Jordan Times, have a somewhat smaller reach (UNESCO, 2015[3]). For their part, television broadcast outlets have likewise grown in Jordan. Currently, 45 satellite television channels operate in Jordan, 17 of which are owned by and directed at Jordanians, 15 of which are private, and two of which are public (UNESCO, 2015[3]).

Radio remains an important channel of broadcast in Jordan, both at the national and regional levels, including 37 FM radio stations operating in Jordan (UNESCO, 2015[3]). In 2000, AmmanNet was established as the Arab world's first online radio station, and in 2015, al-Balad was established as an online community radio channel, dedicated to social and cultural discussion (Fanack, 2017[35]). In addition, online media has expanded in recent years in Jordan, and major outlets include Ammon News, 7iber, Jafra News, Khaberni, Saraya, among others. These outlets are often linked to social and digital media platforms and use a multi-media approach to disseminate news, including Facebook, Twitter, and YouTube, among others.

Despite a growing and diverse media ecosystem, there are a number of systemic challenges that news outlets face in Jordan, including challenges posed to their plurality and independent reporting. Since the adoption of the 2002 Audio-visual Media Law, private outlets have grown considerably, but the state remains a dominant actor in terms of media ownership, including 17 out of 41 radio stations, all terrestrial television broadcasting (e.g. Jordan Television and its Sports channel), and three out of seven of the country's daily newspapers, through ownership of the Social Security Corporation of majority stakes in Al Rai, Addustour and the Jordan Times (UNESCO, 2015[3]). Such a high concentration of state ownership in the sector may affect structural and editorial independence, which can include a lack of autonomy in the way that governing boards and senior staff are appointed, interference in programming and staffing, and slant in reporting.

A related issue is how a lack of media pluralism affects consumer interest, given limits on the scope and depth of coverage on certain issues. A key finding of the peer review mission was that Jordanian media is often side-lined in favour of other Arab-language international media outlets such as Al Jazeera, MBC and Al Arabiya. At the same time, given that a majority of media outlets are located in Amman with few local television stations or daily newspapers outside the capital, UNESCO notes that "the national media is perceived to pay rather little attention to events taking place in remote areas outside of the big cities" (UNESCO, 2015[3]). Given a high rate of access, with more than 90% of Jordanians having access to satellite television broadcast, international outlets are able to capture much of the domestic media market, including BBC, Radio Monte Carlo, CNN International, Al Jazeera and MBC among others.

Individual journalists

The journalism profession and the role of individual journalists in Jordan is largely governed by the Jordan Press Association (JPA). As such, the JPA serves not only as a professional association and union for journalists, but also as the principal accreditor who can officially work as a journalist. In order to qualify as a journalist, Article 5 of the Jordan Press Association Law (1998) notes that certain requirements are necessary, including, among others: (i) Jordanian nationality; (ii) no convictions including misdemeanours or felonies; (iii) enjoyment of full legal capacity; (iv) a qualification from an accredited college or university; and (v) full-time employment for a media outlet registered with the Social Security Cooperation.[20] UNESCO notes that the JPA current counts 1 100 members who work as full time journalists (UNESCO, 2015[3]).

As a result of the current legal framework, a key issue for journalists in Jordan is how the accreditation process functions, including a notable lack of coverage across the profession. As noted, the JPA strictly governs the accreditation process for journalists, making it impermissible to accredit journalists working for foreign outlets as well as most other news outlets outside of the traditional print media. To be sure, JPA membership does not include many journalists working for radio, television, or online outlets, especially those working in "non-news" departments, such as sports, lifestyle, and entertainment (UNESCO, 2015[3]). While the JPA continues to maintain a monopoly on accrediting journalists, it has been estimated that an additional one-third of journalists are working and unable to gain JPA accreditation—leaving them excluded from key protections and benefits (Al-Natour, 2014[36]). While the JPA remains the principle professional organisation for journalists, additional professional associations have made in-roads, including the Society for Jordanian Broadcasters as well as the Electronic Journalism Society, which seek to include more comprehensive and inclusive definitions of what constitutes a journalist.

Linked to challenges with accreditation of journalists in Jordan, additional issues have emerged, including a lack of systematic journalistic training and professionalisation. As noted by UNESCO, six universities provide advanced education in journalism, including Yarmouk, Petra, Jadara, Middle East, Zarqa, and Philadelphia universities, in addition to local civil society organisations such as the Jordan Media Institute (UNESCO, 2015[3]). In addition to these university training programmes, international donors have supported a number of targeted trainings for journalists in Jordan focusing on key competencies. While these programmes have been generally well-received, the dominance of international donors may crowd out other domestic or home-grown training initiatives and have limited sustainability in comparison with the development of national training institutions. Based on the findings of the peer review data collection mission, additional training opportunities and professionalisation programmes are needed as there is a growing perception that many journalists are "aggressive and unprofessional," which in turn undermines their engagement with government and trust among citizens. Such professionalisation programmes would be especially relevant given the lack of "watch dog" organisations that monitor the behaviour of the media against unprofessional media practices.

Media oversight and regulatory institutions

Jordan has a number of regulatory institutions charged with oversight, licencing, and accreditation of broadcast outlets and journalists. The formal broadcast regulatory agency is the Jordan Media Commission (JMC), which was created in 2014. The mandate of JMC is governed by Article 4 of the 2014 Audio-visual Media Law, and includes—among other responsibilities—the ability to: (i) regulate the audio-visual media sector; (ii) study licence applications; and (iii) monitor the work of licensees.[21] However, in terms of the awarding of licenses, the JMC Director is only able to make a recommendation on the "granting, renewal, amendment or cancellation of broadcasting licences" to the Council Of Ministers, which under Article 18, "may refuse to grant broadcasting licences to any entity without stating the reasons for such rejection."[22]

In a similar role, the Telecommunication Regulatory Commission (TRC) was established under Article 6 of the 1995 Telecommunication Law to manage the radio frequency spectrum.[23] As noted by UNESCO, the TRC has a joint jurisdiction with the Armed Forces to manage the radio frequencies spectrum for civilian use, as well as the authority to license the spectrum (UNESCO, 2015[3]). Finally, as noted above, the Jordan Press Association (JPA) is both a professional association representing the interests of journalists as well as the *de facto* authority for accrediting journalists.

Despite the regulatory role of JMC, a number of issues suggest that it does not function as a truly independent agency. To be sure, the government has the sole authority, under Article 6 of the 2014 Audio-visual Media Law, to directly appoint or dismiss the JMC director, which inherently diminishes JMC's standing as an independent agency.[24] Likewise, the revenues collected through the management of licensing are not kept by JMC itself, but rather, returned to the general budget, thus making the JMC dependent on the government for its operating budget. At the same time, "the public has no insight into this aspect of the JMCs decision making regarding licence [or] broadcasters' sources of funding" (UNESCO, 2015[3]). In order to enhance the regulatory independence and transparency of JMC, it would be necessary to ensure that it can independently appoint its leadership, develop independent revenue streams to finance its operations, as well as to make public key application and decision documents in the licencing process.

In terms of other forms of regulation and oversight, including the existence of an ombudsman or other complaint mechanisms, current practices suggest that these functions are underdeveloped. Currently, no ombudsman governing the media and broadcast sector exists in Jordan, nor do individual media organisations have in place internal ombudsmen to hear complaints from citizens. According to Articles 47-48 of the JPA Law, the only system currently in place for receiving complaints is linked to JPA's Code of Ethics and Disciplinary Boards, which allows for complaints to be "submitted to the President of the JPA who then gives the journalist who is the subject of the complaint 15 days to reply" (UNESCO, 2015[3]).

Despite the existence of this system, its efficacy is undermined given that JPA accreditation procedures exclude a large portion of journalists. Moreover, as noted during the OECD peer mission, the lack of a Code of Conduct that applies to a broader range of journalist and adequate oversight mechanisms have led to a persistence of poor journalistic standards.

Government agencies engaging the media

Government agencies in Jordan have increasingly been engaging with media to better inform and engage public audiences. Since 2018, a new National Population Media Strategy (2018-2022) calls for initiatives to align the role of the media with government policy priorities for employment and training of the workforce (The Jordan Media Institute, n.d.[37]). To support these efforts, and as discussed in Chapter 3, the government has established a network of public communicators, known as the *Shabakat Al Natiqeen fil Wuzaraat wa'al Muasasaat al Hukumiya Al Urduniya*, translated literally as "Network of Spokespersons in the Ministries and Institutions of the Government of Jordan." Through this network, the government seeks to reinforce the capacities of spokespeople in key ministries, departments, and agencies as well as to co-ordinate messaging across ministries, departments, and agencies. As confirmed by a recent OECD survey among 14 public entities and MoSMA, findings suggest that 71% of ministries currently have an official spokesperson in place (see Figure 5.6).

While these early efforts have helped to bring together representatives from different ministries—which is especially relevant given the current COVID pandemic response efforts—a number of challenges persist with respect to relations between the government and media. A first issue is the varying levels of capacity and experience of government spokespeople in engaging with journalists. Based on findings from the peer review mission and survey, communication skills are often a challenge for public communicators, who either prefer to avoid the media due to lack of adequate media training or might be off-message if not provided with adequate support. In addition, there does not appear to be a system of pre-briefing spokespeople ahead of contact with the media, whereas pre-established lines and rebuttals are best prepared after preliminary contact with media or otherwise anticipated.

Figure 5.6. Ministries with an official spokesperson

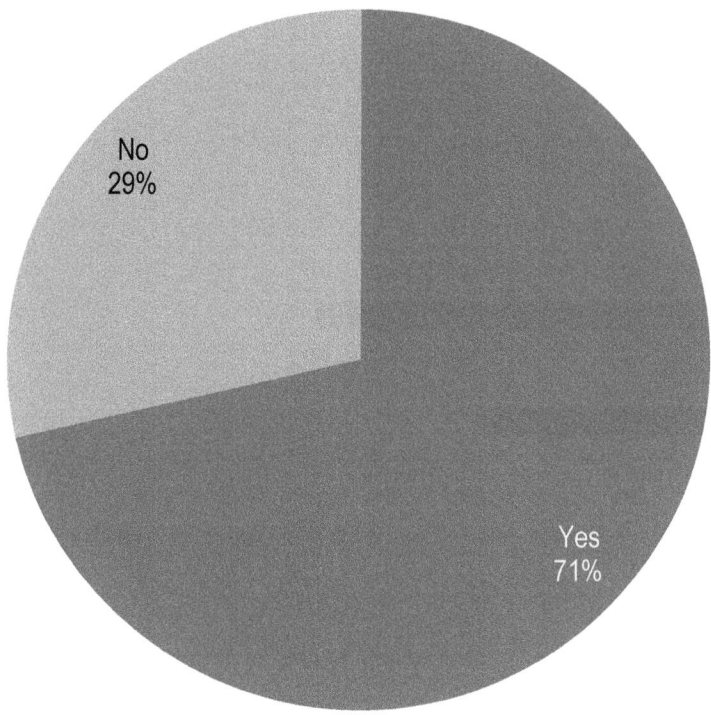

Note: a total of 14 ministries responded to this question.
Source: OECD (2020), Survey for line-ministries in Jordan: Understanding public communication in Jordan.

This lack of familiarity with engaging journalists is exacerbated by practices surrounding the dissemination of information to journalists, including through press releases. Media statements in Jordan are typically made twice weekly, at the end of the day; however, such practices should be avoided because the end of the day is out of sync with the news cycle and catches communications staff with little time to prepare (see Figure 5.7). Information gathered during OECD interviews further indicated a perceived tendency for the government to provide information preferentially to publicly owned media, to the disadvantage of other outlets. Similar challenges exist with respect to the organisation and implementation of press conferences, which appear to be done on an ad-hoc basis. Survey results show that a significant share of ministries primarily grant journalists access to press conferences through direct invitation by the institution, which are also often journalists that the institution has engaged with before. As a consequence, media are inclined to seek information in ways that can create burdens and inefficiencies on spokespeople, with journalists often directly and informally contacting ministers or other government spokespeople, representing a break in protocol and uneven news coverage across outlets.

Figure 5.7. Frequency of press conferences and press releases in Jordanian ministries

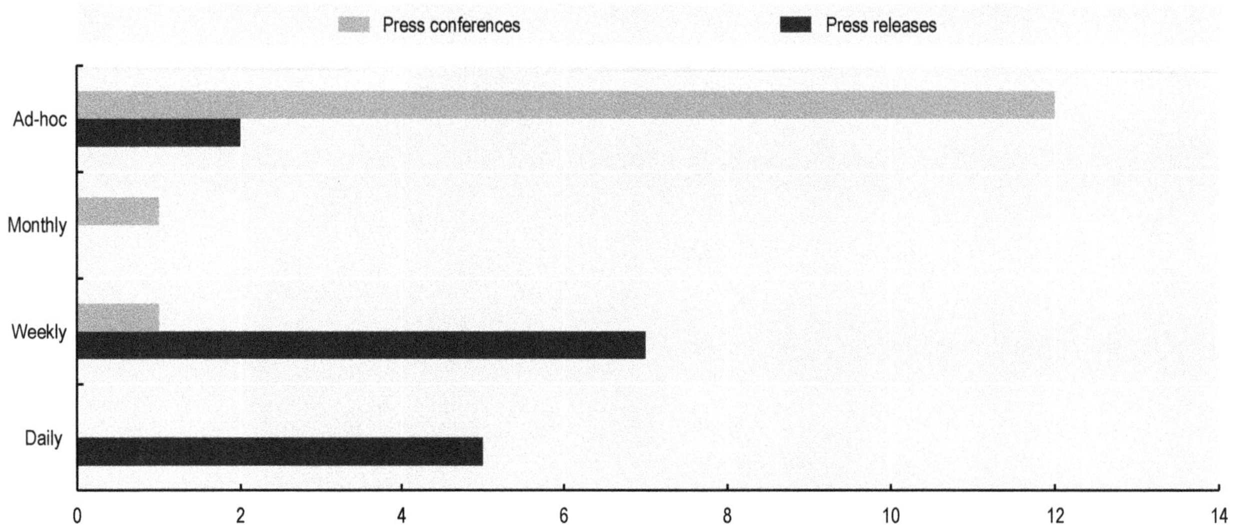

Frequency	Press conferences	Press releases
Ad-hoc	12	2
Monthly	1	0
Weekly	1	7
Daily	0	5

Note: The graphs depicts number of line ministries. A total of 14 ministries responded to this question, selecting the adequate frequency for both press releases and press conferences.
Source: OECD (2020), Survey for line-ministries in Jordan: Understanding public communication in Jordan.

Box 5.2. Public communication skills training for government spokespeople in Jordan

With the Support of the Ministry of State for Media Affairs (MoSMA), two back-to-back training events were organised on 8 and 9 December 2020 in the framework of the Citizens' Voice Project supported by the Foreign Federal Office of Germany. These two trainings helped build the knowledge and skills of over 60 members of the network of public communicators on relevant themes such as strategy development, media engagement and digital communication. This activity supported the government's priorities to professionalise the public communication function and institutionalise practices across core competencies in light of its ongoing restructuring. It also allowed for deeper engagements between attendees to support the future activities of the network of public communicators in the country.

Source: Author's own work, based on OECD (2020[38]), Citizens'Voice: The role of public communication and media for a more open government validation workshop event summary notes.

CSOs, citizens, and other media consumers

As noted above, access and availability to media and information varies among key audiences, given Jordan's diverse set of demand-side actors. The gradual evolution of the media ecosystem in the country has affected the ways in which the public consumes, communicates, and shares information. Notably, Jordan has a high internet penetration rate more than half of the population actively using WhatsApp (78%), Facebook (70%) and YouTube (49%) (Internet World Statistics, 2018[39]). Television (88%) and smartphones (77%) are the most popular channels for Jordanians to consult the news, in addition to a growing share who use Facebook (41%), YouTube (28%) and WhatsApp (24%) for this purpose (NorthWestern University, 2017[40]).

These trends are all the more important when it comes to young people. With youth (aged 12-30) accounting for more than one-third of the population, Jordan is one of the youngest countries in the world

(OECD Development Centre, 2018[41]). As in most OECD countries, social media has become a primary vehicle for engaging with youth, since a significant majority of the target group aged between 18-22 makes use of WhatsApp (82%), Facebook (82%), YouTube (63%) and Instagram (57%) (Northwestern University, 2018[42]).

For their part, civil society organisations are becoming more active in ensuring that media laws and institutions function adequately and that they themselves serve as info-mediaries for key sections of the population. In Jordan, the Centre for Defending Journalists Freedom (CDFJ) is a key interlocutor and advocacy actor, with a mission to "defend media freedom and provide protection to Arab journalists by addressing violations to their rights, providing professional development and ensuring free access to information" (CFDJ, n.d.[43]). Likewise, the Jordan Media Institute has championed the issues of Media and Information Literacy (MIL) as a key policy priority to answer several of the main challenges confronting Jordan, including: responding to disinformation, education, critical thinking, empowerment, ethics, and 21st-century skills (see Box 5.3). These efforts respond to the government's National Population Media Strategy (2018-2022), which has recognised an emerging demographic window requiring an adjustment to educational, training, employment, health and other relevant policies (Jordan Times, 2018[44]).

Box 5.3. Promoting Media and Information Literacy (MIL) efforts targeting youth and civil society in Jordan

The OECD and the Jordan Media Institute organised a series of MIL trainings for a select cohort of young graduates, journalists, and CSOs working on youth issues in Jordan from 11-28 October 2020. The training programme was in high demand by local actors, where the final cohort was formed out of 273 applicants from several regions in Jordan. Over the course of three 5-day training sessions, 45 participants were equipped with relevant tools and skills to identify disinformation and misinformation, as well as to become more critical and responsible consumers and producers of news and information. As one of the outputs of the programme, participants were trained to produce public communication products (e.g. video essays, memes, public service announcements, etc.) to raise awareness of key media literacy issues, including mis- and dis-information, hate-speech, defamation, etc. All 64 memes, 8 comics, and 9 videos produced, including interviews with participants, can be found here: https://bit.ly/3f0ZoWV.

Source: Author's own work.

A key challenge that remains is how the government can best address the changing population demographics in order to ensure that all Jordanians benefit equally from improvements to the media-enabling environment. As mentioned above, a growing "digital divide" has emerged as an additional cross-cutting structural issue in Jordan, which makes equal access to media and information platforms difficult to fully achieve. In this regard, it is critical to understand how certain actors in society can be left behind, which can occur on the basis of socio-economic status, gender, and age, among other determinants. These issues are particularly salient as Jordan deals with an ongoing refugee crisis perpetuated by conflicts in neighbouring countries, a weakened security situation, as well as the economic strains and service delivery challenges brought about by the global COVID-19 pandemic.

Recommendations

This chapter provided an assessment of Jordan's media and information enabling environment in order to determine how it can be best leveraged in support of its ongoing public communication and media engagement efforts. It underlined the importance of a number of political economy issues from structural, institutional, and stakeholder perspectives, which should be addressed in order to best utilise the media to communicate its public policy priorities.

- Use audience insights and channel selection to target messaging and content a wider variety of local stakeholders, which can help to bridge the digital divide to include the poor, women, and youth as key actors in the media and information ecosystem. Where possible, national and local authorities should make use of data on news consumption trends to tailor their selection of audiences and channels. Given disparities in internet access across regions as well as uneven coverage of local issues, it is necessary to ensure that all segments of the population have access to news and public information. While social media can be an effective means to communicate, care must be taken in terms of channel selection to ensure that vulnerable segments of the population can also access relevant information, in particular as digital literacy levels vary significantly across governorates.

- Develop specialised media outreach campaigns on selected issues to specific vulnerable groups through the use of media and information literacy capacity building. With respect to refugees, particular media, information, and public communication campaigns can target these audiences to inform them of the requirements, opportunities, and other relevant information needed for them to better engage with national institutions, programmes, and initiatives. With respect to COVID, Jordan could replicate efforts of other countries who countries have already begun to implement media outreach measures such as campaigns on TV, radio and social media to raise awareness among citizens about hygiene rules and preventative measures to curb the spread of COVID-19 (OECD, 2020[18]).

- Support training and sensitisation efforts related to the recently adopted ATI protocols, which provide clear guidance on classifying, enforcing and managing information. Going forward, technical assistance and capacity building is needed to train Access to Information focal points in various Ministries, departments, and agencies responsible for the implementation of the law as well as training trainers, who can mainstream these provisions across institutions. On the demand side, additional assistance is needed to sensitise and support CSOs, media, research institutions, "info-mediaries," and citizen journalists to submit Access to Information requests. Such efforts can involve the development of guidelines or practical handbooks that inform these actors of their rights, remedies, and expectations with respect to the existing legislation.

- Conduct a comprehensive legal review to better understand the existing laws, regulations, and policies, with an effort to bring them into alignment with international good practices. As has been noted by UNESCO's 2015 Media Development Indicators, there is a large body of laws, regulations, and policies governing the media and information sector, some of which overlap and conflict with each other. In addition to this, efforts can be made to enhance the transparency of regulatory bodies—namely, the Jordan Press Association and Jordan Media Commission—including disclosure of decisions related to accreditation of journalists and licensing of media outlets. Finally, laws related to libel, slander, defamation, and the like should be to be reviewed with an effort to reduce these to civil, and not criminal offenses to be better aligned with international standards.

- Conduct an assessment of the government's efforts to counter mis- and dis-information, including a review of the "Haggak Tiraf" platform. As has been discussed with key stakeholders, the current "Haggak Tiraf" platform on its own cannot reduce the effects of disinformation and a comprehensive assessment is needed to improve its functioning. In this regard, it would be necessary to develop an assessment of the platform with actionable recommendations for increasing its effectiveness in debunking rumours and advancing factual information. This review could be the first of its kind in the region to assess the status quo of disinformation as well as provide support for public institutions to understand the different tools and governance responses available.

- Continue efforts to support transparency and oversight in the media and information sector to reduce the influence of informal practices. In this regard, watchdog organisations such CDFJ should be supported by international and domestic partners in continuing their oversight and related analytics of the sector. Likewise, to avoid the undue influence of "soft containment", media outlets should be subject to mandatory financial and operational disclosures, in line with the existing laws, in an effort to provide greater transparency on their sources of funding.

- Support an enabling environment and financial incentives –including fiscal (tax) incentives, lowering capital requirements for licencing, or providing seed-funding for local outlets—to encourage a plurality of media outlets, including those at the local levels who can better cover issues relevant to local communities. This can involve more direct support to local media outlets, include small local weeklies, local FM radio stations, and other online outlets that cover a broader range of issues pertinent to the wider population.

- Support the further professionalisation of journalists through expanded accreditation procedures and local training institutions. This would include finding alternatives to the monopoly status of the JPA as the core accrediting agency for journalists in order to more adequately include TV broadcast, radio, and online journalists. At the same time, training opportunities can be supported to improve the professional skills of journalists in an effort to better sensitise them to interfacing with government representatives.

- Support the development of strengthening transparency and oversight mechanisms, including the development of an ombudsman or independent complaints mechanism that governs the broader media sector, including all broadcast outlets and journalists. Likewise, it would be equally necessary for the JPA or other professional associations to develop an effective Code of Conduct or Code of Ethics that applies to not only accredited print journalists, but also those working for TV broadcast, radio, and online media outlets.

- Develop the capacities of government agencies that engage the media, including the institutionalisation of standardised procedures and practices, including those for press releases and press conferences. For instance, the government may consider developing comprehensive guidelines for media engagement at all levels of government to ensure a standardised approach, including the collective adoption of the activity grid with the council of ministers as well as digital tools and engaging with the media to foster more co-ordinated measures in all ministries. Likewise, it is necessary to formalise the communications role through the development of an official competency framework.

- Support ongoing government-led Media and Information Literacy efforts to enable CSOs, citizens, and other individuals in becoming informed media consumers. In this regard, a particular focus should be given to learning more about regional, poor, female, and youth audiences, adapting media messaging to their preferred means for engagement. Special attention could be paid to support media and information literacy of these groups through targeting training and outreach activities in an effort to reduce the digital divide.

References

Abu-Shanab, E. and N. Al-Jamal (2015), "Exploring the Gender Digital Divide in Jordan", *Gender, Technology and Development*, Vol. 19/1, pp. 91-113, http://dx.doi.org/10.1177/0971852414563201. [9]

Al Mamlaka (2021), *Director of the Media Authority: A draft law to guarantee the right to information will soon see the light*, https://www.almamlakatv.com/news/65181. [34]

Al-Natour (2014), "A third of journalists are outside the union", http://ar.ammannet.net/news/238892. [36]

Center for Global Communication Studies (2011), *Introduction to News Media Law and Policy in Jordan*, https://repository.upenn.edu/jordan_program/1. [21]

CFDJ (2014), "Status of Media Freedom on Jordan 2014", Center for defending Freedom of Journalists, p. 16, https://english.cdfj.org/cdfj-launches-its-2014-annual-report-on-media-freedom-status-in-jordan-dead-end/. [33]

CFDJ (2011), "Status of Media Freedoms in Jordan, 2011; 2013. Status of Media Freedoms in Jordan, 2013; and 2014. Status of Media Freedom in Jordan 2014: Dead End, p. 16.". [30]

CFDJ (n.d.), *CFDJ Main website in English*, https://english.cdfj.org (accessed on 20 February 2021). [43]

Fanack (2019), *Jordan's Media Landscape*, https://fanack.com/jordan/society-media-culture/jordan-media/ (accessed on 25 September 2019). [7]

Fanack (2017), *Media in Jordan*, https://fanack.com/jordan/media-in-jordan/. [35]

Freedom House (2020), *Jordan: Freedom in the World 2020 Country Report*, https://freedomhouse.org/country/jordan/freedom-world/2020. [31]

Freedom House (2017), *Freedom on the Net 2017 - Jordan*, https://freedomhouse.org/sites/default/files/FOTN%202017_Jordan.pdf. [24]

Fritz, V., K. Kaiser and B. Levy (2009), *Problem-Driven Governance and Political Economy Analysis : Good Practice Framework*, World Bank, Washington, DC. [27]

Global Centre for Democracy (2016), *RTI Rating*, https://www.rti-rating.org/country-data/Jordan/ (accessed on 13 April 2021). [19]

Government of Jordan (2018), *Fourth Open Government Partnership National Action Plan (2018-2020)*, https://www.opengovpartnership.org/wp-content/uploads/2019/01/Jordan_Action-Plan_2018-2020.pdf. [22]

GSMA (2018), *State of Mobile Internet Connectivity*. [12]

Helmke, G. and S. Levitsky (2004), "Informal Institutions and Comparative Politics: A Research Agenda", *Perspectives on Politics*, Vol. 2/04, pp. 725-740, http://dx.doi.org/10.1017/s1537592704040472. [26]

Internet World Statistics (2018), *Middle East Internet Users, Population and Facebook Statistic in 2018*, https://www.internetworldstats.com/stats5.htm (accessed on 26 September 2019). [39]

Jones, D. (ed.) (2001), *Censorship: A World Encyclopedia*, Routledge. [23]

Jordan Media Monitor (2012), *Soft Containment and its Effect on the Independence of Media*. [32]

Jordan Times (2018), "Government raises minimum wage, hikes taxes on tobacco, telecom services", http://bit.ly/2ItIPqH. [13]

Jordan Times (2018), "Jordan launches media strategy to invest in 'upcoming demographic window'", http://www.jordantimes.com/news/local/jordan-launches-media-strategy-invest-upcoming-demographic-window%E2%80%99. [44]

JPA (2014), "Third report on Press and Media Freedoms Indicators in Jordan", pp. 9-12. [29]

Jütting, J. et al. (eds.) (2007), *Informal Institutions: How Social Norms Help or Hinder Development*, Development Centre Studies, OECD Publishing, Paris, https://dx.doi.org/10.1787/9789264039070-en. [28]

Middle East Monitor (2019), *Government survey: Extreme poverty in Jordan at 15.7%*, https://www.middleeastmonitor.com/20190409-government-survey-extreme-poverty-in-jordan-at-15-7/. [10]

NorthWestern University (2017), *Social Media Use in the Middle East*, http://www.mideastmedia.org/survey/2017/interactive/social-media/who-use-the-following-social-media-platforms-facebook-whatsapp-twitter-instagram-snapchat-youtube-etc.html (accessed on 26 September 2019). [40]

Northwestern University (2018), *Media Use in the Middle East*, http://www.mideastmedia.org/survey/2018/interactive/online-and-social-media/who-use-the-following-social-media-platforms.html# (accessed on 26 September 2019). [42]

OECD (2020), *Citizens' Voice: The role of public communication and media for a more open government in Jordan event summary notes*, https://www.oecd.org/gov/open-government/citizens-voice-in-jordan-validation-workshop.pdf. [38]

OECD (2020), "COVID-19 crisis response in MENA countries", *OECD Policy Responses to Coronavirus (COVID-19)*, OECD Publishing, Paris, https://dx.doi.org/10.1787/4b366396-en. [18]

OECD (2020), *Engaging Citizens in Jordan's Local Government Needs Assessment Process*, OECD Public Governance Reviews, OECD Publishing, Paris, https://dx.doi.org/10.1787/c3bddbcb-en. [5]

OECD (2019), *Institutions Guaranteeing Access to Information: OECD and MENA Region*, OECD Publishing, Paris, https://dx.doi.org/10.1787/e6d58b52-en. [20]

OECD (2017), *Towards a New Partnership with Citizens: Jordan's Decentralisation Reform*, OECD Public Governance Reviews, OECD Publishing, Paris, https://dx.doi.org/10.1787/9789264275461-en. [6]

OECD Development Centre (2018), *Youth Well-being Policy Review of Jordan*, EU-OECD Youth Inclusion Project, Paris, http://www.oecd.org/dev (accessed on 26 September 2019). [41]

Poushter, J. (2016), "Internet Access Growing Worldwide but Remains Higher in Advanced Economies", http://pewrsr.ch/1TwX4H2. [15]

Rawabdeh (2019), "The "Your Right to Know" platform", *Al Jazeera*, http://www.jordantimes.com/news/local/govt-launches-%E2%80%98right-know%E2%80%99-app-bid-combat-rumours. [25]

Silver, L. et al. (2019), *Mobile Connectivity in Emerging Economies*, Pew Research Center, https://www.pewinternet.org/wp-content/uploads/sites/9/2019/03/PI_2019.03.07_Mobile-Connectivity_FINAL.pdf. [14]

The Jordan Media Institute (n.d.), *National Population Media Strategy 2018-2022*, https://www.jmi.edu.jo/en/national-population-media-strategy-2018%E2%80%932022. [37]

The Kingdom of Jordan's Department of Statistics (2019), *Jordan Population and Family Health Survey 2017-18*. [4]

TRA (2019), *Telecommunications Market Indicators (Q1/2018-Q4/2018)*, Telecommunications Regulatory Commission. [1]

UN WOMEN (2020), *Gender and the digital divide in situations of displacement: The experiences of Syrian refugee women in Al-Azraq and Al-Za'atari camps*. [17]

UNESCO (2015), "Assessment of media development in Jordan". [3]

UNHCR (2020), *Syria Regional Refugee response portal*, https://data2.unhcr.org/en/situations/syria/location/36. [16]

World Bank (2021), *MENA Crisis Tracker*, https://documents1.worldbank.org/curated/en/280131589922657376/pdf/MENA-Crisis-Tracker-June-27-2021.pdf. [11]

World Bank (2020), *Does the internet reduce gender gaps? The case of Jordan*, http://documents1.worldbank.org/curated/en/282451584107082621/pdf/Does-the-Internet-Reduce-Gender-Gaps-The-Case-of-Jordan.pdf. [8]

World Bank (2019), *World Development Indicators*, https://databank.worldbank.org/source/world-development-indicators. [2]

Notes

[1] Constitution of the Hashemite Kingdom of Jordan, Amended 2011.

[2] Universal Declaration of Human Rights.

[3] International Covenant on Civil and Political Rights.

[4] Arab Charter of Human Rights, Article 32, 2004.

[5] Convention on the Rights of the Child.

[6] Euro-Mediterranean Association Agreement.

[7] Sanaa Declaration on Promoting Independent and Pluralistic Arab Media.

[8] Law No. 47 on Securing the Right to Information Access, 2017.

[9] While this analysis seeks to present an overview of key laws and regulations, it should not be considered as an exhaustive legal analysis, as this is a highly complex sector with multiple overlapping laws and a dynamic legal framework. To be sure, there are more than a 20 laws and statues in Jordan that directly govern the media, including among others: The Press and Publications Law (1998) as amended, Penal Code (1960) as amended, State Security Court Law (1959) as amended, Contempt of Courts Law (1959), Protection of State Secrets and Documents Law (1971), Jordan Press Association Law (1998) as amended, Jordan Television and Radio Corporation Law (2000), Provisional Law for Audio-visual Media (2002), Prevention of Terrorism Law (2006) as amended, Access to Information Law (2007), Jordan News Agency Law (2009), Cyber Crimes Law (2010).

[10] Press and Publications Law No. 10 for the year 1993, published in the Official Gazette No. 15391, p. 311, 17 April 1993.

[11] Law No. 8 of 1998, published in the Official Gazette No. 4300, p. 3162, 1 September 1998.

[12] Department within the former Ministry of Information, which then was set under the PMO and subsequently merged with the Audio-Visual Commission to form the Media Commission.

[13] Law No. 15 of 1998, published in the Official Gazette No. 4304, p. 3745, 1 October 1998.

[14] Provisional Law No. 71 of 2002 for Audiovisual Media.

[15] Amended Press and Publications Law no. 30 for the year 2012.

[16] The 2015 Cybercrimes Law.

[17] تعرف حقك (haggak.jo).

[18] The survey is based on questionnaires distributed to 582 journalists and managers from daily and weekly newspapers.

[19] The As Sabeel journal recently switched to a sole online model.

[20] Article 5 of the Jordan Press Association Law (1998).

[21] The Jordan Media Commission was established on 30 April 2014 by Law no.17 for the year 2014.

[22] Article 18(b) Law of the 2014 Audiovisual Media Law.

[23] Telecomunications Law, no. 13 for the year 1995, published in the Official Gazzette on 1 October 1995, edition No. 4072, p. 2939.

[24] Article 6(b) Law of the 2014 Audiovisual Media Law.

www.ingramcontent.com/pod-product-compliance
Ingram Content Group UK Ltd.
Pitfield, Milton Keynes, MK11 3LW, UK
UKHW051345130526
12444UKWH00021B/305